Well

Well

Well

Well

Well

Well

God Still Heals Today

Jay W. West

Well, Well, Well
Copyright © 2015 by Jay W. West

Anointed 2 Go MdM
Bellevue, NE

Cover & Key Images © Copyright byDesign 2015, Cynthia Pleskac

Image contribution by: ZigaC, Hydromet,Focusstock.

All rights reserved. This book is protected by the copyright laws of the United States of America. This book or any parts therein may not be reproduced, distributed, copied or transmitted in any form, not electronic, mechanical or any other means, or stored in a database or retrieval system without the prior written permission of the publisher. The use of short quotations or occasional passage copying for personal or group study is permitted and encouraged.

Unless otherwise identified, all Scripture quotations are from the New King James Version. © 1982 by Thomas Nelson, Inc. Used by permission. All rights reserved.

Scripture quotations marked (AMP) or "The Amplified Bible" are taken from THE AMPLIFIED BIBLE. Old Testament copyright © 1965, 1987 by The Zondervan Corporation. The Amplified New Testament © 1958, 1987 by The Lockman Foundation. Used by permission.

Scripture quotations marked (KJV) or "King James Version" are taken from the King James Version of the Bible. Public Domain.

Scripture quotations marked "Latin Vulgate" are from the Latin Vulgate Translation of the Bible. Public Domain.

Scripture quotations marked (MSG) or "The Message Bible" are taken from THE MESSAGE. © 1993, 1994, 1995, 1996, 2000, 2001, 2002. Used by permission of NavPress Publishing Group.

Scripture quotations marked (VOICE) or "The Voice" are taken from *The Voice Bible* © 2012 Thomas Nelson, Inc. The Voice™ translation © 2012 Ecclesia Bible Society.

WORLDWIDE PUBLISHING GROUP
Your Multi-Platform Publishing Partner
(713) 766-4272

Ebook: 978-1-68411-602-7
Paperback: 978-1-68411-613-3

For further information, to contact Jay West regarding speaking engagements, or to order resources:

Please email anointed2go@cox.net or go to http://www.anointed2go.com.

Endorsements

There is such power in the healing testimony. I expect many reports of people being healed as they read this book.

Sid Roth,
Host, "It's Supernatural!"

Jay West's new book is a wonderful work on healing from a man who has much experience and knowledge of the ministry of healing. I believe it can be a benefit to those who read it, and I highly endorse the ministry of Jay West.

Dr. Randy Clark
Global Awakening

I met Jay West for the first time at the "Global Awakening Conference" in Orlando. We had coffee together with his son Jason. There was no question this man that I was meeting for the first time face-to-face carried a mantle on him for healing and the presence of God. We enjoyed a few hours together that seemed to pass so quickly. I was pleasantly surprised when he asked me to endorse his book, only because we had just met. This, I think, speaks to what kind of man Jay West is, and without hesitation I said, YES!

When you hold this book in your hand, I believe it will be the beginning of a great encounter with God. *Well, Well, Well* is written a little bit like the Bible. It's full of God's Word and stories that validate objective truth. There is no doubt that Jay wrote this book with much prayer and life experience. This is one book that can and will change your life as you apply the nuggets within it. It's not just a book to read; this book has the potential to transform your life. It's relevant and revolutionary to your walk with God.

I've met a lot of great leaders throughout my Christian walk, and I don't throw flowers very easily. What so impressed me about Jay West was that he was a down-to-earth kind of man. He was real and full of the love of God for people. It's for that reason I was honored to endorse this book. It wasn't just about the book, but the man who wrote it.

If you're hungry to experience God in a new way, let this book help you on your journey. It is cutting-edge, present truth, from God's heart to yours. Now, let the journey begin, because your life is about to change!

Pastor Sam Hinn
Orlando, Florida

Imagine! Really, just imagine what it would be like if you discovered that Jesus not only still heals people today just as He did when He walked the earth—but that He intends to heal you… and that He plans to use this very book to prepare you for that healing! Got it? I believe this is that book to build your faith and to teach you what the Lord is doing with healing right now on the earth, at the moment you're reading these words. And this book is about what Jesus really is about to do for you and many of your friends and relatives… That's right… He's about to heal you! And He's doing it through the most unlikely human vessels—regular people who look just like you! In fact, when you're finished reading this book by Jay West, you may literally be screaming, "God, *use me to heal people* like the stories in this book! Jesus—please use me!"

Now, as Jay will tell you in this book, "If you are sick and battling cancer, fibromyalgia, or arthritis, You need a fresh word from God….You don't want some person praying, 'If it be Your will, Lord.' You want that person to stand in faith in agreement with you in power and wisdom with an understanding that the

Bible is full of manifested healings, because Jesus Christ is the same yesterday, today, and forever (Heb. 13:8)."

Let me end with this: If you haven't done so already, get this book! And you better get one as a gift for a friend too.

Steve Shultz
Founder, THE ELIJAH LIST and BREAKING CHRISTIAN NEWS

Well, well, well, Jay West has done it again. For those of you who know Pastor Jay West's prior three books, you already know that he uses an engaging, almost conversational style while combining a solid biblical foundation with practical anecdotes and testimonies. *Well, Well, Well* continues with this tradition. In this book Pastor Jay addresses the topic of healing. Drawing upon his own experiences in confronting illnesses and health challenges in his own personal life and the many testimonies of how God has successfully used him and his ministry to bring healing to others, Pastor Jay crafts a book that is personal, compelling, and inspiring. If there is one thing that characterizes Pastor Jay, his ministry, and his books, it is his desire to bring ministry down to earth so it will be user-friendly for everyone. In this book, Pastor Jay does exactly that, inspiring you to want to get involved in Jesus' healing ministry yourself. Pastor Jay shows how scientific/clinical medical practice and the healing power of the Holy Spirit can and do work incredibly effectively together. I am reminded of the words of Jesus ben Sirach in the thirty-eighth chapter of the apocrypha book of Ecclesiasticus, which says:

> Pray to the Lord, and he will make you well. Confess all your sins and determine that in the future you will live a righteous life. Offer incense and a grain offering, as fine as you can afford. Then call the doctor—for the Lord created him—and keep him at your side; you need him. There are times when you have to depend on his skill. The doctor's prayer is that the Lord will make him able

to ease his patients' pain and make them well again. (Ecclesiasticus 38:9, Good News Translation)

Pastor Jay's book provides a practical, easy-to-read-and-follow framework to integrate the best practices of clinical medicine with our faith that Jesus heals today and wants to bring heaven to earth. This book will make you want to move beyond your comfort zone and begin to move forward in healing the sick in the power of the Holy Spirit. Like Pastor Jay, you will want to see all become well. I heartily recommend this book to everyone.

Rev. Frederick P. Duncanson, MD, FACP, FIDSA
Infectious Diseases physician and clinical researcher
Episcopal priest, Diocese of New York
Chaplain Order of St. Luke Northern NJ Chapter
Chaplain for Healing, St. Michael's Church, Wayne, NJ

Contents

Endorsements 5
Dedication 11
Acknowledgments 13
Making an Appointment (Foreword) By Jason West 15
Initial Consultation 17
Preliminary Diagnosis 19
First Checkup **Healing Waves, Abiding Presence** 23
Second Checkup **Three Years of 24/7 Pain** 37
Third Checkup **Fresh Manna, Fresh Manifestation** 45
Fourth Checkup **A Stone's Throw Away** 55
Fifth Checkup **Aye Aye—Eye Eye!** 65
Sixth Checkup **Effective Energy** 75
Seventh Checkup **EE2** 85
Eighth Checkup **This Is a Great Day to Get Well** 93
Ninth Checkup **Intercession, Revelation, Manifestation** 103
Tenth Checkup **More on Intercession** 115
Eleventh Checkup **Unusual and Uncommon Un-Methods** 125
Twelfth Checkup **Eating Disorderly** 133
Thirteenth Checkup **Wells, Shacks, and Cisterns** 143
Fourteenth Checkup **Supernatural Perseverance** 155
Closing Prayers **By Jason West** 165
Other Products Available from Anointed 2 Go MdM 167

Dedication

This book is dedicated, in part, to some of our doctors who, over the years, have been a blessing to our lives and faithful to their healing vocations. This list is not inclusive, but does reflect the significance in our lives of those listed:

- ✓ Dr. William Boyce—my family doctor when I was a child in Escondido, CA.
- ✓ Dr. O'Doyle Dannenberg—my family eye doctor in Escondido, CA.
- ✓ Dr. Martin Van Court Bradley—our dentist in the Houston area. Our son Jason has "Bradley" for his middle name due to Dr. Bradley's influence in our lives. People often say that Jason has a great smile, and we always respond, "Well, of course, he was named after a dentist. What would you expect?"
- ✓ Dr. Marc Spector—another dentist friend of ours in Houston, TX.
- ✓ Dr. Magdy Rizk—The doctor who delivered Jason in Houston, TX, on December 28, 1991. There is a story about him in my first book, *Downloads from Heaven*.
- ✓ Dr. Mark Woodruff—our family physician in Omaha, NE.
- ✓ Dr. Brian Brockman—our family chiropractor in Omaha, NE.
- ✓ Dr. Walter Wood—Emergency Room, Bellevue, NE.
- ✓ Dr. Andrew Trainer—urologist in Omaha, NE.
- ✓ Dr. Lannie Weak and Dr. Courtney Molettiere—our family dentists in Omaha, NE.
- ✓ Dr. Sue Rodgman—a member of our church where I was a pastor in Hugoton, KS.
- ✓ Dr. Jack Cooper—our eye doctor in Dallas, TX, and member of our church at the time.

Dedication

- ✓ Dr. Fred Duncanson—personal friend from New York.
- ✓ Mary Steffen—nurse practitioner in Chicago and my wife's sister.
- ✓ Dr. Luke, who wrote the books of Luke and Acts in the Bible.

Acknowledgments

Thank you to:

- Diane West—Love, patience, and thirty-five years of marriage

- Gary Peterson and Jason West—Editing

- Cynthia Pleskac—Cover Design

- Dr. Randy Clark—Book endorsement

- Dr. Fred Duncanson—Ministry intercessor and contributor; book endorsement

- Pastor Sam Hinn—Florida limo, personal meeting, and book endorsement

- Sid Roth—Personal dinner and book endorsement

- Steve Schultz—Elijah List prayer team invitation and book endorsement

- Jason West – Foreword, Son, Author and Worship Leader

- Pastor Jim Hart—Overseer and book contributor

- Dr. Bill Jackson—Mentor and book contributor

- Jim West—Brother and book contributor

Dedication

- Jason West—Son, worship leader, author, and book contributor

- Meg Michener, Pastor Bill Wise, and Pastor Shane Rootes—Book contributors

- Eddie Smith and Bill Vincent—Publishing

- Members and friends of Kingdom Encounters, Omaha, NE

Making an Appointment (Foreword)
By Jason West

Very few readers can say they've known the author of a book their whole lives, but I can! And because I've known him my whole life, I have had a front row seat to observe and also be involved in the healing ministry that God has graced my dad with. And let me tell you: It is real, and it is authentic. He doesn't pray or minister for show. He ministers from the heart, and he equips others to do the same. It is not about making a name for himself; it is about leading people to the name of Jesus.

One of the titles I remember my dad considering for this book was "Un-Hyped Healing." That is truly an accurate description of how he ministers and how the Lord has used him over the years. He is very humble and sensitive in his approach to praying for others, praying lovingly and gently, yet firmly and with compassion. I believe this approach both honors the Lord and the people being ministered to, and it leads to many glorious and miraculous testimonies—many of which you will read in this book.

I believe the reason for this can be largely attributed to how my dad endeavors to live by the reality that Jesus only did what He saw His Father doing (John 5:19). So if Jesus lived that way, it is a good indication that we should too. It is not about following a certain method, as if there is a one-size-fits-all approach to healing ministry. Rather, it is about following Jesus. And Jesus ministered in all kinds of different ways in all kinds of different situations. That is because each person is different, and each circumstance is unique. My dad has often stated that Jesus prayed for six different blind people in six different ways. So the key is to find out what

Jesus is doing, and then do that; rather than just doing something because we've always done it.

The topic of healing can encompass many things. A particular theme that will stand out to you in this book is that there is value in the healing process, whether that process involves medical or miraculous healing—or a combination of both. Jesus healed people instantaneously; He healed people through a process; and He even utilized the assistance of medical professionals. All are biblical, and all can be effective in their own right. Another thing you will discover as you read is that healing can encompass many facets of life, including physical, emotional, and spiritual. And God wants us to be healthy in all of these areas.

With these things in mind, let me conclude by stating that my dad is the same in the public eye and in private. He has prayed for my healing many times when I was sick, injured, or even had a simple headache. He was always gentle; he always sought to pray how Jesus led him to pray in that moment; and he never hesitated to seek the appropriate medical care for me when needed—but he always started first with prayer. I remember many occasions when I began to quickly feel better as a result of that prayer. I can recall other instances when the prayer opened the door for a strategy to help solve the problem, and when we implemented that strategy, the healing came quickly. And I know that he didn't simply pray for me; he taught me how to pray too, because he was always interested in equipping others to do the work of the ministry.

So as you read this book, get ready to be encouraged but also equipped to do the work. I believe God will use this book in your own personal healing journey, and He will use it in your journey of learning how to pray for others and see God's healing power manifest in their lives too. Well, Well, Well... Are you ready to jump in?

Initial Consultation

Thank you for choosing to read my book. I believe you have made a good choice, and I pray that this fun approach and interpretive rendering between medical healing and supernatural healing will provide a hunger for fruitful encounters with God. You have permission to get well at any time while reading this book!

My motive in writing books is to get the message out about how wonderful God is and how He so desires to work for you and minister through you, just like He has for me. One of my theme Scriptures is centered on Ephesians 4:11–12, where the five-fold offices of ministry are given by Jesus, as recorded by Paul, for the purpose of equipping and training the people of God to do the work of the ministry, rather than just doing it for them. So many church congregations have the attitude that the pastors and staff are hired to do the work of the ministry, but this is not the mandate of the New Testament. Keep reading, and you will learn to discern how God can work through you just as well and effectively as any pastor or church leader. This discovery can literally change your whole perspective on your present ministry.

Instead of using the word *chapter*, each section is called a "Checkup," to align with the theme highlighted in the forthcoming Preliminary Diagnosis. Another word for checkup is *examination*, and in each chapter we examine what the Word of God says about healing. A further reason for using the word *checkup* is because almost every time I've concluded a prayer for healing I declare that there is a miracle when you check. My prayers are directed up toward heaven, so using the word *checkup* has a companion meaning, both from a medical perspective and that of actually checking for supernatural results after praying for someone.

Unlike my previous three books, this one has no study guide at the conclusion of each chapter. This is intentional because

I really dislike methods and work hard at doing only what I see the Father doing. Jesus did the same when agreeing to this practice in John 5:19 and 30. So as you read this book, please stay focused on what the Lord is sharing with you and telling you to do. If He gives instructions, step out in faith and do what He asks you to do, responding with faithfulness and gratitude that He has chosen you to carry out His assignment within your sphere of influence. Isaiah 1:19 declares that if we are willing and obedient, He will give us the good of the land. Boldness is a byproduct of knowing Jesus and being filled with His Spirit.

Someday when I get to heaven, I want the Lord to say, "Well done, good and faithful servant" (Matt. 25:21). I don't want to hear Him just say, "Well, well, well, look who showed up." Personally, I enjoy it when God shows up with me today. Receiving Jesus as your Savior and Lord includes two important components. Having Jesus in our lives provides the opportunity to get to heaven from earth when we die, but also gives us the option to access heaven while still living on earth. In what is often called The Lord's Prayer, these words were penned for all eternity: "Thy Kingdom come, Thy will be done, in earth [in your location right now where you are] as it [already] is in heaven" (Matt. 6:10, KJV, emphasis added). Remember, with God's Word and power, there is no expiration date.

Lord, I pray that Your Kingdom will come to every person reading this book, that new dimensions of truth will be secured, that new waves of glory will be experienced, and that we will all learn how to flow in Your presence and in Your Kingdom operation. Let the encounters begin. If you agree, say, "Well, well, well! I am well!"

Preliminary Diagnosis

Part of my goal while writing this book was to recognize that in addition to supernatural healing, God can and will use medical doctors to promote healing. There is a passage in the Bible at Acts 28:8–9 that describes both of these options. Let's use it as a heavenly prescription for the rest of this book. Since many prescriptions are written with Latin terms, I will list the verses in Latin and then in English:

> *contigit autem patrem Publii febribus et dysenteria vexatum iacere ad quem Paulus intravit et cum orasset et inposuisset ei manus salvavit eum quo facto et omnes qui in insula habebant infirmitates accedebant et curabantur* (Latin Vulgate)

> And it happened that the father of Publius lay sick of a fever and dysentery. Paul went in to him and prayed, and he laid his hands on him and healed him. So when this was done, the rest of those on the island who had diseases also came and were healed.

In verse eight, the Greek word for "healed" is *iaomaio*, but in verse nine the Greek word is *therapeuo*. That second word is where we get our English word *therapy*, implying that the healings in verse eight by Paul were supernatural, while the ones in verse nine could have been more therapeutic with Luke employing either natural or therapy-related medical care to those who were touched by Paul.

But since I am not a biblical language scholar, I consulted a good friend of mine, Dr. Bill Jackson, who has functioned as my mentor and who is also an author and leads his own ministry called Radical Middle Ministries out of Corona, California. Here is his response to my question about these two words that are both translated "healing":

Hi Jay,

I checked out your options and concluded that this interpretation is possible. Historical narrative is assessed for its probability. In this case, while the two words *iaomai* and *therapeuo* are basically synonyms for healing, *therapeuo* can have the connotation of "care for" or "cure." Cure could easily have the shade of meaning of medical help. But given that Luke here implies that the healings were immediate, this might mean that some needed care afterward in some way.

Given the number of people that had come forward for healing prayer, even though Luke is using hyperbole (overstating the case to make the point), Paul would have needed help. Luke's presence there as a physician would lend itself to his involvement as one of Paul's teammates, not just in "doctoring" but also in the laying on of hands for healing. I would say that it is very possible that Luke was involved in the healing process. I'd also say this moves this interpretation over into the realm of very possible and maybe even probable.

In Ben Witherington's commentary on Acts, he says, "It is not impossible that Luke was involved in some way." Witherington is a top notch scholar who teaches at one of the best seminaries in the country, a Methodist school in Wilmore, Kentucky, called Asbury.

Now that you have read this interesting possibility, you may even be saying to yourself, "Well, well, well, isn't that interesting." This authentication sets the tone for both insights to be included and explored in the narrative of this book.

I hope you will share this book with your ministry and medical friends alike, letting them know that there is a balanced approach to healing written and practiced with the intended purpose of helping others get well.

First Checkup
Healing Waves, Abiding Presence

Recently on the way home from church, I saw a sign for an estate sale, so I decided to go check it out. After purchasing a couple items, I came out to the car and saw an open house sign across the street, so I decided to venture over and look at the house. My wife Diane and I love to look at open houses to get decorating and gardening ideas. As I walked into the house, the realtor greeted me and started to share about the house. He offered to let me roam the house, but I encouraged him to come with me and point things out. Immediately, I noticed he was limping. When we got to the stairs to descend to the basement, he then gripped the handrail with both hands and walked very slowly and sideways down the stairs.

At the bottom, I inquired as to what was wrong with his feet, and he shared that he had some growths that had been surgically removed but had grown back a couple of times. I casually yet intentionally mentioned that I thought God could heal his feet. Then I proceeded to share a testimony of how I had once prayed for a man at a restaurant who had a bone spur and how God healed him in the parking lot of the restaurant. I added with an encouraging smile that God likes to heal at restaurants and at open houses, and the realtor replied that he would take anything at this point. So I jumped at the chance and offered to pray. My prayer was less than thirty seconds in length, as I declared his healing. Then, I shared that there is a miracle when you check and asked him to walk across the basement floor. He did that and immediately told me that there was substantially less pain. I had him walk again, and this time the pain was almost completely gone.

I then asked him to go up and down the stairs, and he went right up with a normal gait and came right back down in a natural way too. We went back upstairs, and he went walking on the hardwood floors, just amazed that he had no pain. He then told me that he was Presbyterian and had been taught all his life that healing had passed and stopped with the end of the apostolic age. He went on to say that he never believed in healing for today, and then with a very long pause, he added, "Until today." He received a gentle wave of healing from Heaven that demonstrated how God's abiding presence is still available today and did not pass with the apostolic age. One of the reasons it did not pass is because the apostolic age is not over either, but that is another subject.

God has enabled me to minister in the area of healing now for many years, but with gradual increase over the past few years, seeing quicker responses, faster healing, and more rapid recoveries, as healing impartations have been shared, prayed, taught, and received. I believe God wants all of us to be well. Thus, I have used a little phrase, "Well, Well, Well," as the title of this book to assist you in promoting a healthy approach to biblical teaching on healing.

Integrate and Disintegrate

My goal is to integrate faith and disintegrate the hype and the sensationalism that sometimes accompany the demonstrations and manifestations of the Holy Spirit. This hype is at times promoted by individuals who have been mistakenly impressed somehow to think that they are the reason that these things are happening, rather than giving the glory back to God for all that He has done through them. But I have to admit to you up front that even though I am seeing large percentages of people I pray for getting well, and while I have experienced a measure of successful healing manifestations, I am really just an apprentice and continue to learn and grow in my understanding in these areas. It is an area for ongoing growth, and I am learning more and more about healing almost every day. While I am disappointed when I don't see someone get well, I am also elated at the number of people who do get well and keep on pressing in for more. This is just like the surfer who, when he misses a wave or completely wipes out, will still go back and try to catch the next wave.

I work hard at ministering in a low-key fashion, trying not to draw attention to myself, but to promote Kingdom life and encounters with God while seeing Jesus get lots of credit, honor, adoration, devotion, and adulation. Simultaneously, there are times when God just shows up in a huge way and the manifestations happen like rapid fire from a weapon that no one can control (nor would they want to). It's during these times that we see God's Kingdom on display, which is His way for that particular moment to draw more people to Him. It's His deal, His party, and His event, and I am just along for the ride. Jesus is the agenda!

The Waves of God

This rapid fire, or super-manifested presence of the Lord, is often experienced in worship services or revival meetings where the presence of the Lord seems to be coming in waves, sometimes at a very fast and steady pace. This happens almost like storm waves during the high tide on a beach. Storm waves can quickly erode away a beach, leaving little sand and/or large divots and trenches where the sand that embraced the water once was smooth. In the same way, God's presence, flowing in waves like the wind or ocean, often erodes away anything ungodly, cleansing the vessel of the disease and providing a new foundation on which to stand. All that can be shaken will be shaken and all that is firm and built on the rock will remain.

It is during these times that we often see God's Kingdom on display, which is His way at that particular moment to draw more people to Him. In the natural, many people do not pray when the weather is sunny, calm and peaceful, but let a storm start to brew, and many will call upon the name of the Lord as if they have personally known Him for many years.

These wave-filled moments are designed by God to build momentum, much like a new wave increases in force and velocity far out from the shore until it crashes with amazing force and impact on the shore. It is during these encounters that someone might utter under their breath, "Well, well, well, this can't be God. Look at the carnage." But I counter and would equally state with a different emphasis, "Well, well, well, look at what the Lord has done. Let's examine the fruit of the wave before we wash our hands of the experience." Charles Spurgeon said, "I have learned to kiss the wave that slams me into the rock of ages." Now that is an excellent perspective.

Sometimes the waves are gentle, calm, and tranquil, much like the ones pictured on the front cover of this book. God knows when we need a big ride on a large wave and when we need to glide peacefully along in solitude and just let the water gently lap at our being. The wave, regardless of the intensity, helps us participate in the Kingdom of God on earth. Sometimes we need to wait on God to move just like a surfer waits to ride the next big wave. These are often times of preparation and meditation with a desire for His presence to carry us to the next level. While the Kingdom of Heaven is a place, the Kingdom of God is an experience, and every surfer values both the place and the experience.

I asked my older brother and former surfer Jim West to write something about riding the waves. I hope you will hang ten and enjoy his informative and entertaining presentation on surfing.

How to Catch a Wave

The Beach Boys said it in their hit tune from 1963:

"Catch a wave and you're sitting on top of the world."

And according to them, here's all one needs to do:

"You paddle out, turn around, and raise, And baby, that's all there is to the coastline craze."

First Checkup: Healing Waves, Abiding Presence

Well, when that song came out, I was just starting high school and also just starting to surf. Trust me, as far as catching a wave, I don't think the Beach Boys had a clue. And that's understandable. According to an Internet search, it appears that drummer Dennis Wilson was the only one who had ever done any surfing. It even seems that Beach Boy leader Brian Wilson had an almost phobic fear of water.

Here are some of the realities I found about catching a wave when I was a "grom" (surf lingo for young, inexperienced surfer). First off, I have to get a board. In the early '60s, there were no short boards, and the long ones cost about $150 and up, which was a lot of money in those days. The used one I bought was 10' 3" long and almost three feet wide.

The next thing I had to do was somehow transport that monstrosity to the beach. I lived in northern San Diego County about 20 miles from the nearest surf spot. That meant getting it there by car. Today, in the age of short boards, kids that live close enough can get their board to the beach on a bike or even under their arm on a skate board. However, since skateboards as we know them today weren't even in existence in 1963, I had to use a car. That meant a set of roof racks because, even if I had a pickup truck or a station wagon (preferably a "Woodie"), my giant ten-foot board would not fit in the back very well.

Then, when I got it to the beach parking lot, there was the issue of getting my board from the car to the sand. That sucker was really heavy. I could barely get my arm around it and could only grasp the "rail" by the tips of my fingers. Obviously, I couldn't make it too far without frequent rest stops. The alternative was to put it on top of my head and walk with it that way. This was certainly painful and didn't make for quick progress either. Then came the challenge of the long steps down to the beach because of the cliffs at the best surfing spots. Having that heavy board bouncing up and down on my head as I traveled down the steps was not fun at all. And the thought of having to come back up the steps after a day of surfing was discouraging to say the least. But I would persevere and somehow make it to edge of the water. I was sure that every "Wahine" (beach girl) was watching me in awe. A "Wahine" is a Polynesian word for young lady.

Now, I would put my board down on the sand and prepare to apply the obligatory surf wax. WAX??? Oh, shoot! I left it in the car. Oh, well...back up the steps to retrieve it.

Finally, after quite a bit of time rubbing on the wax (remember, this is a ten-foot-long board with a lot of surface area—in some ways, it reminded me of a small aircraft carrier), I still needed to squeeze myself into my undersized wetsuit somehow, unless it was summertime, in which case regular swim trunks would do. These eventually evolved into "jams" and later into "board shorts" with their troublesome Velcro closures which could cause

First Checkup: Healing Waves, Abiding Presence

multiple bodily problems. Even in the summer, when a wetsuit wasn't needed, it was customary to put on a thin but very tight rash guard to prevent skin discomfort from all the wax I had ground into my board. At this point, some sixty to ninety minutes since leaving my home for the beach, I was ready to enter the water and follow the Beach Boys' advice to "paddle out, turn around, and raise."

But wait a minute, before I do that, I better survey the situation. Where are the best waves breaking? How many other surfers are already out there? Is there a less crowded alternative with acceptable waves? What's the best route to get there? With all those questions answered, now it was finally time to enter the water and catch that wave. I knew those Wahines were still watching me, so I better get going.

But wait another minute. If the surf is really any good today, then the corollary is that it is creating a lot of "white water" from waves that have broken. This minefield of broken waves must be traversed in order to get out where the good "break" is happening. Keep in mind that in order to have the full experience, I must also navigate my aircraft-carrier-sized board with me. So I run as best as I can, carrying my giant board into the water. When I get about knee deep in the water, I throw the board in front of me, toss myself on top of it and paddle furiously.

It isn't long before a large white-water wave is rushing toward me, threatening to knock me clear back to the beach or maybe even up the stairs to the parking lot. Nowadays, the surfers with short boards can execute a move called a "duck dive," which basically means to rise up on the board on your hands and feet, push the nose under the oncoming wave, and follow your board underwater to resurface on the backside. Obviously, this doesn't work well with a 10' 3" board. The alternate technique, called a "turtle roll," involves pushing one side of my board down with one arm while pulling up on the other side with the other arm, thus turning my board belly and skag (fin) up. Then, I hold on for dear life while upside-down underwater as the huge wave passes over and tries to rip the board from my hands. If it succeeds in doing so, it probably takes it all the way into the sand because leashes (which attach your board to a foot) had not been invented in 1963. Even if they were, having a leash on a board this big would probably result in a broken ankle.

After a lot of hard work, paddling, turtle rolling, etc., I finally make it "outside" (beyond where the waves are breaking). This is a calm area to relax and reflect on my adventure. It is in this area that I just sort of abide with nature and enjoy the presence of the gentle up and down motion of smaller waves. I sit on my board, catching my breath from breathing so heavily because of my previous exertion as I watch other surfers make their way out. The more experienced ones make it look as easy as the Beach Boys say it is. Rather than lying flat on their stomachs with waves pounding in their faces, they get up on their knees to paddle out. From this vantage point, they are much better equipped to judge the waves rushing toward them, and they look a whole lot cooler. Unfortunately, my knees and ankles do not take well to being mashed into the hard wax on my board, and I find that I am much more easily swept off my board if I try to paddle while kneeling on my board. I hope the watchful Wahines are accepting of this.

After an appropriate period of rest, it is time to paddle in a little bit to where the waves are actually breaking. I watch the swells, pick one that looks good (not too big and not too small, with a good shape), position myself strategically, and begin paddling toward the shore. As the swell moves under me, I feel it take over my giant board like it was a match stick. I no longer need to paddle as the wave is now carrying me. I have paddled out, I turned around and raised. I caught a wave, and I'm "sitting on top of the world." It sure wasn't as easy as the Beach Boys said, and I hope the Wahines are still watching.

"So take a lesson from a (not so) *top-notch surfer boy... Just get away from the shady turf And baby go catch some rays on the sunny surf*

You gotta catch a wave and you're sittin' on top of the world."[1]

Capacity

My brother, in addition to catching the wave, wanted to catch the attention of the Wahines. For those of us who love God, we want to catch the attention of the Lord. The Bible says in

Corinthians that we make it our aim to be well pleasing to the Lord. There's that word *well* again, and obviously this time it means to have the added energy of being motivated, enthusiastic, and favorably approached in an advantageous manner. But to be well pleasing with a deep, deep sense of appreciation, with deep faith, is also rightly used to demonstrate our desire to attract the attention of the Holy Spirit.

Our desire should be to enlarge our capacity for more of God. Let's briefly analyze that word *capacity*. "Capa-" is the prefix from which we get our word *cape*. This cape is the red cloak that a bull fighter uses to provoke the bull to charge. The bright red tint, combined with the movement of the cape, attracts the bull. As this prefix "capa-" evolved in etymology through our current language, other words, such as chapel and sanctuary, unfolded. In essence, we have become a chapel or sanctuary for the Holy Spirit to move in waves to attract others to Jesus. Obviously, the second word from capacity is *city*. Our goal is to attract the Holy Spirit to our city, and we do that as we ride the waves that God puts in front of us in any private or public sector that He chooses. If God is not sending a wave of His presence when you are in your favorite store, then don't try to make one happen. However, if He does send a signal that He wants to do something, don't chicken out and ignore it. We choose to embrace what God is doing, not what He is not doing.

Well Stated

Perhaps you have heard the phrase, "Well, well, well. What do we have here, then?" This is an old phrase used on occasion by police officers in Great Britain upon the discovery of people engaging in criminal acts. It dates back to the Victorian era.[2]

I have noticed that if one's tone of voice goes down the melodic scale as that person declares those three words, "Well, well, well," then the tone of voice often indicates sarcasm, disgust, and disapproval. But if the tone of one's voice goes up the scale, then the words imply being impressed with approval, perhaps with

First Checkup: Healing Waves, Abiding Presence

a level of surprised, unanticipated anticipation of greater things to come. (That was a mouthful, for sure!)

Let me assure you, though, that the tone and vocal articulations will always end each chapter with an incline, with levels of approval coupled with expectation. This book is written on the upswing and follow-through of a great athlete growing in his or her game rather than the disgruntled voices of so many who will declare, "Well, well, well," as a sign of their ongoing disapproval. Philippians 1:10 speaks of approving things that are excellent, and I share my confidence with you that everything about God is excellent. Psalm 37:5–6 from the Message Bible declares, "Open up before GOD, keep nothing back; he'll do whatever needs to be done: He'll validate your life in the clear light of day and stamp you with approval at high noon."

But I am using this phrase, "Well, well, well," as a play on words, with the primary emphasis pertaining to physical, emotional, and spiritual healing, adding the accentuation of using the word *well* three times instead of just simply stating the person is now well. This book will also emphasize starting well and finishing well with a standard of excellence.

Proverbs 15:31 in the Message Bible makes this declaration: "Listen to good advice if you want to live well, an honored guest among wise men and women." In all my books, including this one, I emphasize John 5:19, which says that Jesus only did what He saw the Father doing. If you want to live well, then simply do what you see the Lord doing, take His advice first, and ignore the naysayers. If someone tells you it can't be done, it is often more of a reflection of their limitations than yours. Just stay focused on riding the wave that God has created for you, and don't be swayed to go the world's ways.

If you do this, regardless of the cost, then following Jesus will enable you to sing and shout with the great hymn writer, "It is well with my soul!"

Whether you are rich or poor, drive a nice car or a clunker, have great influence or live a more solitary life, after being ill in some capacity and then getting better, it is always such a joy to declare, "I am healed; I am well. Thank God!" Who doesn't appreciate it when the flu finally leaves or the symptoms of a cold are no longer lingering? Everyone appreciates when the cast comes off, the surgery is complete, the Novocain wears off, the radiation is over and the prescriptions no longer need to be taken.

There is great joy when we no longer need to make appointments with the specialist. It is equally wonderful to cancel multiple tests, discontinue x-rays, shut off the drilling at the dentist, or have the braces removed and to be able to smile while declaring, "I am glad that is over!" Being able to live healthy and well is such a delight. What exhilaration, euphoria, and excitement are generated at those special times!

As you continue to read, you will gain biblical insights that will equip you to believe for the impossible, coupled with plenty of wonderful testimonies challenging you to reach for more of God. By doing so, God will take your life and ministry to another level, while promoting the Kingdom of God and helping others to do the same. Remember, the Kingdom of Heaven is a place and the Kingdom of God is an experience. Bible study without Bible experience is pointless.

Look at how this plays out in Ezekiel 18:5–9 in the Message Bible:

> Imagine a person who lives well, treating others fairly, keeping good relationships—doesn't eat at the pagan shrines, doesn't worship the idols so popular in Israel, doesn't seduce a neighbor's spouse, doesn't indulge in casual sex, doesn't bully anyone, doesn't pile up bad debts, doesn't steal, doesn't refuse food to the hungry, doesn't refuse clothing to the ill-clad, doesn't exploit the poor, doesn't live by impulse and greed, doesn't treat one person better than another, but lives by my statutes and faithfully honors and obeys my laws. This person who lives upright and <u>well</u> shall live a full and true life. This is a Decree of God, the Master. (Emphasis added)

First Checkup: Healing Waves, Abiding Presence

In Luke 8:48 (MSG) Jesus offers this simple advice: "Live well, live blessed!" A definition of the word *blessed* is, "To be empowered to prosper and be in control of any situation, regardless." Thus, the passage from 3 John 2–4 really impacts us with this declaration: "Beloved, I pray that you may prosper in all things and be in health, just as your soul prospers. For I rejoiced greatly when brethren came and testified of the truth that is in you, just as you walk in the truth. I have no greater joy than to hear that my children walk in truth."

There is an obvious connection between walking in truth, being in health, and prospering. The first connection is that your soul is prospering. This book will explore those options and godly principles under the guise of the words, "Well, well, well." Proverbs 10:29a indicates this truth in 3 John with this blessing: "God is solid backing to a well-lived life." That well-lived life is available through Jesus Christ.

The Good Life

As I write this book, I currently live in Omaha, Nebraska, and the slogan on most signs as you enter Nebraska from another state says, "Welcome to Nebraska, The Good Life." I grew up in San Diego, California, where the weather is much milder than Nebraska, and I made up a little saying that goes like this: In California, thirty-two degrees was freezing but in Nebraska, thirty-two degrees is melting. For this California boy, the good life does not include cold weather, but I have learned to adjust and appreciate my assignment here in Nebraska.

Please trust me when I say that, while many things are good in Nebraska, they don't compare to what a true good life experience is by knowing and walking with Jesus on a daily basis. His Kingdom is truly the good life that will amaze and astound you with awesome experiences as you become a son or daughter of the King.

Acts 17:28 expresses this truth quite well: "For in Him we live and move and have our being, as also some of your own poets have said, 'For we are also His offspring.'" Being an offspring means that I have access to the family home, all the assets and partnerships of my Father, and all the advantages of living in His presence. Psalm 103 challenges us not to forget the benefits of living in His Kingdom. As a child of God, I have the run of the house!

An offspring is an offshoot from the larger well, so the water that is in my Father's well is also flowing out to me, establishing a new well and a new reservoir that may produce a gentle, peaceful stream or a turbulent white-water rafting experience. So with this wave of Holy Spirit well water, let's join together to look for some gushers in the spiritual well business! Now, who wants to surf or go tubing? The next wave might be small or large, gentle or powerful, but whatever the size or intensity, it will benefit us since it is from our Father. Are you ready? Another wave of His presence is about to hit.

Second Checkup
Three Years of 24/7 Pain

I remember working in the backyard on a warm June day, pulling weeds from around our flowers, when suddenly I suffered a keenly piercing pain in the lower left side of my abdomen. It was one of those things that you remember, as it was so sharp and acute that it nearly knocked the wind out from me. I recalled sitting on the grass for a moment, wondering what it could be, and then surmising that it somehow must have been related to the new blue sports drink I had consumed the previous day.

After I rested a bit, I resumed pulling weeds, only to have it happen again. This time, I decided to stand up, thinking I had been on my knees and bent over so long that I must be having some sort of related stomach cramps. But soon after standing I had another pointed pain in the same area, so I headed indoors to see if we had any stomach antacids or liquid medicine that I might take to help remedy this profound assault on my digestive system. While I was looking for the medicine, the pain continued. But I found some liquid antacid, swallowed it quickly, and decided to lie down and take a nap.

In a little while I did start to feel slightly better, and I soon fell asleep, only to wake up later with more of the same acuminate pain. I remembered thinking to myself, *No more odd colored sports drinks for me!* I would not venture out and be that brave in the future.

Little did I know that the initial pain on that June summer day in Texas was the beginning of three very long years of battling not only that pain but a host of other symptoms too. This would be the beginning of a very intense and arduous healing process, which included hundreds of people praying for me, learning to eat and exercise in ways that contributed to better health, multiple doctor visits and medical tests, along with experimenting with many health food products as well.

This was a test of endurance for me as an individual, a trial which often brought me to my knees in desperate prayer, with many anxious thoughts and turbulent contemplations of what my future would hold as I battled day in and day out for my healing. The cause of this pain was most likely something called IBS, which stands for Irritable Bowel Syndrome, a disease that strikes far more women than men and, at the time I contracted it, was labeled as being incurable. I was offered tranquilizers to help me sleep, but I refused to even have the prescription written, as I did not want to become dependent on sedatives to get any rest.

Regretfully, I did not keep a journal during this time of physical anguish, but I do remember many of the details as if they happened yesterday. The lower GI tract test with barium enema, along with the air contrast, is one that sticks vividly in my mind. Having non-related hernia surgery in the midst of these pain episodes is but another detail that I cannot forget. Then suffering new pain after the surgery and undergoing ultrasounds and other tests to determine if, by chance, the operating staff left something in me or made some sort of medical mistake is yet another indelible memory.

During this time, I learned that some foods I thought were good for me, such as salads, were actually contributing to the pain I was experiencing, because leafy vegetables are difficult to digest and sometimes get caught up in the lower intestines and colon area. This is certainly true for most nuts, corn, and a variety of other foods. I further discovered that beets are the number one colon food and that large portions of protein would help eliminate the pain for small periods of time. I also learned that various colon flushes and dietary aids did absolutely nothing to assist me with the on and off again constipation, bloating, coupled with diarrhea and even some bleeding. I was in a tough season with a medical deficiency pill that was not easy to swallow.

Comfort Flows Through Us

Then, on top of that, my wife Diane and I had been trying to have children for several years, and nothing seemed to be

Second Checkup: Three Years of 24/7 Pain

working. We were sad about this, and it just contributed to this painfully prolonged period in my life that, in many ways, I would like to forget. But in other ways, it contributed BIG time to an appreciation for the healing ministry that flows through me from the Holy Spirit. I learned deeper levels of empathy and sympathy for those with chronic pain and can more easily identify with those who are struggling with long-term illnesses.

Second Corinthians 1:3–4 gives a vivid demonstration of how this works: "Blessed be the God and Father of our Lord Jesus Christ, the Father of mercies and God of all comfort, who comforts us in all our tribulation, that we may be able to comfort those who are in any trouble, with the comfort with which we ourselves are comforted by God." I don't have to experience every disease known to mankind to comfort someone else. All I have to do is rally the comfort that I gained and appropriated through the Holy Spirit and then take that same comfort and extend it to someone else who needs it. This is a transferable principle that frequently appears in the Bible. Matthew 10 exhorts us to freely give just as we have freely received.

Revelation 19:10 further encourages us to access the prophetic when hearing a testimony with this Scriptural thought: "The testimony of Jesus is the spirit of prophecy." When we listen to testimonies, instead of just nodding our head with a churchy *amen*, we can actually agree with the testimony as a prophetic word from God that He wants to do a similar miraculous thing in our lives. As in the comfort being shared from 2 Corinthians 1 in the above paragraph, we don't have to align ourselves perfectly with the testimony to receive a specific word from God in our lives. We just open the gate and give entrance to His prophetic words in our lives for a similar thing to happen to us. That's how amazing and powerful God's Word is. Psalm 119:130 actually says that the entrance of His words gives us light for our life.

God has done so many wonderful things as a result of these episodes, and they definitely served to prepare me for what was coming. You might even wonder if God actually sent them for that purpose as a season of preparation. I would unequivocally say no, as I don't believe God sends sickness or illness to anyone in and under the New Testament covenant of grace. But He definitely helped me learn some important medical structures, along with improving my personal compassion for others who are in any pain, battling any disease, and with whom I happen to have the privilege of praying for their personal healing.

As I previously mentioned, I was offered prescription strength sleep aids but turned them down, and I rarely had any problems falling asleep, which in and of itself was a God-sent miracle, for sure. On the occasion that I would wake myself up crying, my compassionate wife would gently pray for me in English and in the Spirit, and I would soon fall back asleep. Thank you, Diane.

In those days, I was on staff at a Houston church that had a large staff and congregation. Because of the size, there were multiple caring folks who frequently asked me how I was feeling. I always tried to be truthful and honest in my appraisal of the intensity of the pain, but then I intentionally would include some verbal testimony of God's Word or some Bible verse that was meaningful to me, to set the stage for what I believe God wanted to do in my life. In a sense, I was anticipating a wave of God's healing presence. As the Bible articulates, we have the option to choose life or death and to speak life or death. I could have responded and just said, "I guess since the doctors said I would have this for the rest of my life, I have no choice." But instead I decided I would bring forth a word of hope to every person who inquired about my health. I attempted to rely on the Word of God for my final answer in this medical dilemma, not the doctors' opinions. There are medical facts, and then there is biblical truth. Sometimes they line up, and sometimes they don't. When they don't align together, I will always choose the Word of God. I admire all my doctors, but there is a reason why they call it a "practice."

Declarations are Rally Points

Job 28:22 expands this biblical rudiment further with this charge: "You will also declare a thing, and it will be established for you; so light will shine on your ways." During my time in

Second Checkup: Three Years of 24/7 Pain

Houston, those declarations were coupled with lots and lots of prayerful requests too; whereas, now I normally just declare and speak healing. And I try to model and teach this as often as I can.

Jesus told us in Matthew chapter ten that we are to heal the sick. I honestly can't find a place where Jesus prayed for healing. Over and over, He just spoke to the situation and extraordinary life manifested, which replaced the ordinary life that had previously occurred. These declarations seem to be rallying points for the Holy Spirit, Who was on Jesus to provide power for the supernatural healing. The Holy Spirit is also on us with power to bring help and healing to others (see Luke 4:18–19).

The power of prayer became very real to Diane and me during those times, as we recognized that with an incurable disease it boiled down to the fact that all we really had was God. He definitely came through for us, too. Not only did He heal my pain and deliver me from the disease, but He also gave my wife and me a wonderful son, which I will share about in a later chapter. (I also wrote about it in more detail in my first book, *Downloads from Heaven*.)

You might remember from reading the dedication to this book that our son's name is Jason Bradley West, named in part after our dentist in Houston, whose name is Dr. Bradley. Dr. Bradley was a tremendous source of encouragement and a diligent, faithful prayer partner during most of these battles, so it seemed appropriate to include the name Bradley in the name of our son as well. You just can't beat having strong friends in Jesus. Proverbs 17:17 declares, "A friend loves at all times, and a brother is born for adversity." Those three years were definitely times of adversity, as the forces of hell seemed to fight against us on so many fronts.

Now as many years have passed, we have a better understanding of why Jason's delayed birth into our family was actually the plan of the Lord. The timing of the Lord was perfect as Jason grew older and started leading powerful worship and prayer ministry with me when I traveled to various churches. This ministry springs from the depth of Jason's heart and soul due to his increased tempo for worship and prayer. We actually refer to him in our new church plant called Kingdom Encounters as the MP3. "M" is for Music, and "P" is for prayer. I can't tell you what the 3 is for because we don't actually know either, but it sounds cool.

Twice in First Timothy, Paul instructed Timothy to fight the good fight of faith. This command occurs in 1:18 and also 6:12. When God says something twice in a limited amount of space, you know it is important. I know we did not always measure up to the "good fight" standards, but we did conclude the title bout in that way, and with the help of Jesus, we won. I often tell people that it might feel like you are laid out on the ground, dusty and dirty, perhaps even bleeding, but if you won, then you know it was a good fight.

After that long battle and fight was over, I later learned that a lady in our church named Linda Griffin prayed for my healing every single day of those three long years. She did not reveal that information or share it with me in any way until after I was completely healed. For someone to take that initiative and to do that for anyone is truly amazing and humbling too. I don't know that I have actually prayed for any of my friends every single day for three years. This truly is a selfless act of kindness and perseverance that is rarely seen in our busy world. I am very grateful for Linda's commitment and prayer consignment that she undertook as a servant for Jesus. There is a lesson in there for all of us.

On June 1, 1991, the pain vanished, along with all the other symptoms. What the doctors declared as impossible to heal, God responded with the opposite prognosis. I remember thinking on that day, *Wow, so this is what it feels like not to have pain.* It was an exhilarating feeling that I really had not had for three very long years.

A cool thing happened in 2013, when on June 1, I was preaching a message at a local church where I was leading a healing service, and the title of the message was, "This is a Great Day to Get Well." It was the twenty-second anniversary of when my healing manifested for me in my body, and it truly was a great day to get well. Actually, every day is a great day to get well, and as you read more of this book, you will undoubtedly discover how

Second Checkup: Three Years of 24/7 Pain

this is true. In Chapter 8 you will learn more about how any day is a great day to get well, and in chapter 13 you will discover some practical information about how to expand your capacity for even more of God in your life. But you have permission to get well right now too.

Every healing for every person is significant, from a small pain issue to a complex medical problem. God is in a good mood and wants to heal you today; in fact, He is in a good mood every day. He is better than Arby's fast food chain restaurants in that God is good mood spiritual food every day.

There is much more that could be shared about this chapter of my life, and some of it is actually revealed in my first three books, but suffice it to say that I will never stop proclaiming how God saved me from this terrible disease and healed my body. I will never stop thanking Jesus for His healing power. And for those who think that Jesus doesn't heal anymore, well, well, well, you are just too late. Someone forgot to give that memo to Jesus because He definitely healed me.

Third Checkup
Fresh Manna, Fresh Manifestation

Dear Pastor Jay,

My greatest pleasure in life is not only to receive God's blessings for me and my loved ones, but to give the glory and honor back to Him because I know that all good things come from our Father.

Four years ago, I went to see an eye specialist for the severe dry eye problems I developed after a botched LASIK surgery. My biggest regret in life was having that surgery. Not only did I still need glasses for my vision, but I can't even describe all the pain I've been through with the dry eyes I developed from the surgery. It got so bad that even though I put drops in my eyes multiple times during the day and ointment in both eyes at night at bedtime, *I was afraid of waking up in the morning because I'd always have stabbing pain in both eyes when I first opened them.*

At that first eye appointment, the doctor made several suggestions for what to do about my dry eyes, all of which I'd already been doing. It was at that time that I discovered that I have glaucoma. I hadn't even turned 50 yet, so the doctor was very worried that I had glaucoma at such a young age. One year ago, I met you when you were speaking at a women's Aglow conference I was attending. I got up the courage at the end of the prayer session to come up to you and ask you to pray for my dry eyes. You did, and from the next morning on to present day, my eyes have not had that intense stabbing pain upon waking that they did before. I am so grateful for your prayers, but I know that you were just the vessel and that it was Jesus who healed me. Praise God!

This past year, more testing has shown that the glaucoma has gotten worse in both eyes. I am allergic to beta blockers, so I am limited in the kind of eye drops I can use. Before each eye doctor visit, I pray to God, saying I trust Him completely and am at peace with what the doctor says. I have asked for you to pray for my glaucoma to be reversed also, although I know that is not medically possible. Recently, when I came to Omaha to attend the conference where you were speaking at Calvary Lutheran, I specifically had you pray for my healing of the glaucoma. (Nothing is impossible with God!)

The most incredible thing is happening now that I can't explain. Even though visual field tests are showing that I am getting bigger holes in my vision with the advanced glaucoma, I am actually seeing so well now that many times I don't even need glasses to drive!! I feel in my spirit that God is saying to keep trusting in Him to take care of me. It must be supernatural from God, because in the natural world my vision would keep getting worse instead of better. I will continue to trust in what my Lord and Savior has in store for me, no matter what.

~Meg Michener

Third Checkup: Fresh Manna, Fresh Manifestation

Manna

Now, there is an example of fresh manifestation apprehended through the application of fresh manna.

The word *manna* is the Hebrew term for the supernaturally provided bread that was fed to the children of Israel who were wandering in the wilderness for forty years. The word *manifestation* is a word used in biblical language to describe the revealing of God's power in ways that declares who He is and what He can do. Manifestation imparts heavenly realities to earth for the purpose of revealing truth, demonstrating power, and making Jesus famous. Okay—granted, He is already famous, but to some He remains completely hidden and unknown.

We also discover that the word *manna* literally means, "What is it?" The children of Israel looked at this bread-like material that would rot in one day if not consumed and simply asked, "What is it?" I am sure they tried many ways to prepare it so that it appeared tasty, but I am thinking that after even forty days of eating the same thing, it probably lost a lot of interest, yet it remained one of two primary foods for this very large group of people to eat.

On the other hand, Jesus is referred to in the Scriptures as the Bread of Life, and His taste value will never diminish, as the Bible declares, "Taste and see that the Lord is good" (Ps. 34:8). There is a goodness factor to Jesus that always satisfies, and we don't have to try to figure out new ways to make Him more appealing. We just accept and receive Him for Who He is, and the Holy Spirit does the rest. It's really pretty simple. Isaiah 55:2 adds, "Why do you spend money for what is not bread, and your wages for what does not satisfy? Listen carefully to Me, and eat what is good, and let your soul delight itself in abundance." Many try to work their way into salvation or buy their way into the Kingdom, but it is not for sale. The fresh Bread of Jesus is given freely to us who will receive Him.

Acts 4:29–31 offers us this information:

"Now, Lord, look on their threats, and grant to Your servants that with all boldness they may speak Your word, by stretching out Your hand to heal, and that signs and wonders may be done through the name of Your holy Servant Jesus."

And when they had prayed, the place where they were assembled together was shaken; and they were all filled with the Holy Spirit, and they spoke the word of God with boldness.

I can just hear everyone talking who was near this event, as the verbal response probably went up the scale in marvel and wonder declaring, "Well, well, well!" This has to be one of those times when those who observed these things could not remain silent. After all, that was the prayer, wasn't it? That they would speak with more boldness? So God answered with a manifestation that shook them to the core, as they truly wanted to share the fresh Bread of Jesus with others, plus see accompanying signs and wonders to back up the preaching of the Word of God.

Delight Contains Light

Psalm 37:4 encourages us to delight ourselves in the Lord and He shall give us the desires of our heart. Then Psalm 119:105 declares some remarkable truth about the Word of God: "Thy Word is a lamp unto my feet and a light unto my path." What a glorious and delightful description. I intentionally used the word *delightful* because the prefix "de-" means to come down from, so when something is delightful regarding the Word of God, it's as if the Word of God is full of light coming down to us. As we download the light of the Lord in our lives by delighting in Him, we then set ourselves up to receive the Word of God that adds the illumination in the place that we need it. Let me explain.

Third Checkup: Fresh Manna, Fresh Manifestation

When Psalm 110:105 says that the Word of God is a lamp unto our feet and a light unto our path, we really see and appreciate two different types of lighting effects. The lamp unto our feet is similar to the reading lamp in your living room, bedroom, or office that lights just enough for you to see in the immediate surroundings. But the light on the path is like a larger or brighter halogen light in your backyard basketball court that lights up the whole area and often reflects even further out. It could easily be compared to stadium lights at an outside football or baseball stadium. This is a much larger illumination and is for the purpose of giving us the big picture.

So there are times in your life and mine when God shows us a little and other times he reveals substantially more. Either way, His delight in us is reciprocated by us as we delight in Him. In chapter two, I quoted to you from Job 28:22, and I will now paraphrase it to you: If you declare a thing, it shall be established for you, and God will shine on your ways. So His spotlight is on you when you step out in faith and declare something based on faith and founded on the Word of God. And we can then expect the manifestation to be right there in the light as well.

Second Corinthians 4:6 from the Amplified Bible brings added depth to this discussion with this verse: "For God Who said, Let light shine out of darkness, has shone in our hearts so as [to beam forth] the Light for the illumination of the knowledge of the majesty and glory of God [as it is manifest in the Person and is revealed] in the face of Jesus Christ (the Messiah)." As the light shines to us, we experience the manifestation of Jesus in our midst, and He brings with Him more than enough options to provide solutions, answers, wisdom, healing, provision, and many other choices as the Light of God shines brightly on us.

The problem is that too many believers are eating stale bread in the dark. I've met a few pastors who have told me they never hear from God, they never encounter God's power, and they don't have a clue what to preach to their congregations. I've had others tell me that they download sermons off the internet and read them to their congregations. Wow, just what I want: a canned, used sermon or message from a pastor, being read to me. This would be kind of like a homeless person digging for scraps of food in a dumpster. Scraps of food do not make a meal, and food found in a dumpster is not fresh. Hungry believers are entitled to fresh manna and not stale bread. When stale bread is served, people walk out and ask each other, "Do you have any idea what the pastor was talking about? Did you understand his message? I don't see how that relates to my life at all."

These comments are common in some congregations, and it isn't any wonder why people are leaving so many churches and looking for answers in different venues. We are to be delightful carriers of the Light as we help others lighten their personal load. We take great joy in knowing that we have moved from darkness into His marvelous Light. These experiences and personal encounters with God create testimonies and opportunities to share His word personally and effectively with others.

I am further convinced that if Jesus walked the earth today and began to multiply bread and fish for large crowds, many would have stood up and complained with possible comments like these: "I'm a vegan," "Is there mercury in that fish?" or "What about the gluten content?" I think in many of today's churches, people are often more interested in explaining away the possibility of a miracle before it happens. Canned sermons just perpetuate this problem.

I don't quote the King James Version of the Bible often, but Matthew 22:29 translates better in this version: "Jesus answered and said unto them, 'Ye do err, not knowing the scriptures, nor the power of God.'" That is exactly what is happening in many churches. The pastors and the people do not really know the Scriptures and the power of God. As a result, people leave asking, "What was that?" Similar to what manna means: "What is it?"

If you are sick and battling cancer, fibromyalgia, or arthritis, the last thing you want is some canned message off of the Internet. You need a fresh word from God, with fresh anointing, coupled with the fresh breath of God in your situation. Anything short of fresh manna and a fresh manifestation is unacceptable. You don't want some person praying, "If it be your will, Lord."

Third Checkup: Fresh Manna, Fresh Manifestation

You want that person to stand in faith in agreement with you in power and wisdom with an understanding that the Bible is full of manifested healings. While these were written to us by the writers of old, they are active and present today just like they were in Bible times, because Jesus Christ is the same yesterday, today, and forever (Heb. 13:8).

Fresh Bread

Can you imagine Jesus trying to read some ancient manuscripts to the people who were listening to the Sermon on the Mount? His words were fresh and full of power, life, and promises downloaded directly from heaven. Even if your body is well, and you don't need any healing, and other areas of your life are flowing nicely and you don't need any supernatural manifestations, your spirit still needs to be fed. To have stale, old, crusty sermons that were received by some other means than a "thus saith the Lord" will only turn your stomach sour to the things of God. It won't be long until you start looking for sustenance from some other supernatural source, but the rest of those places are all rooted in darkness. Jesus is the true Light of the world, and it is in Him that you live, move, and have your being.

If you are in a church where the pastor is reading *Reader's Digest* quotes to you and sharing sports stories, never referring to the Scriptures, then run from the church as fast as you can and find yourself a good Bible-believing, Bible-preaching church that embraces what Jesus is doing today. Look for Kingdom life and Kingdom promises that are actually happening. Seek out a place where people are fed the Word of God and it is producing change in their lives. Don't sit in a place dying of spiritual hunger. Find a church home that fills you up and leaves you hungering for more and more of God, where it is a shame not to talk about God.

It is interesting that in the natural when you abstain from food, you grow hungry pretty quickly; but in the spiritual realm, if you abstain from God and then get around those who love being with God, you will do anything you can to change the subject so that you don't have to talk about Him or listen to others talk about Him. These are polar opposites, yet often very true.

The other side of the coin reveals a similar picture. When you eat a large meal, say at a backyard barbecue, and after two hamburgers, two ears of corn, a couple of brats, baked beans, chips, drinks, and appetizers, someone then brings out the apple pie and ice cream with some watermelon on the side, you will probably be like most people and say, "I'm so full. I think I will just wait awhile." But when you get filled up with God, all you want is more of God. You just want to eat and eat and talk about Jesus, be in His presence, and get as much as you can. People in this process are often referred to as being hungry. Even though they don't know it yet, they are hungering and thirsting after righteousness, because nothing else satisfies.

There is a warning in 2 Timothy 3:5 that tells us some people and leaders will have a form of godliness but will also deny the power, and that we are to stay away from those people. Have you ever stopped to think why that is? These people can know the liturgy, quote the creeds, know when to say *amen*, clap, and raise their hands, but they simply deny the power. That can be the supernatural manifested power of God or it can be the power of the Word of God. Again, if your pastor is reading canned sermons to you, this is probably a good sign that he or she is denying the power of God.

If your small group leader depends more on a secular book for sharing in the group than on the Word of God, that could be a red flag to you that it is time to change small groups. And without the power of God to back it up, the only manifestation you will get when you need a touch from God is one that is rooted in darkness and makes what you have feel even worse, rather than providing an avenue for improvement, prosperity, healing, and restoration. That's what Jesus came to do. He came that you might have life and have it more abundantly.

The Bible declares to us that people will speak out of the abundance of what is in their heart. If someone hardly ever wants to talk about God or can't even stand bringing God up in a conversation, there is a pretty good chance that what he or she is

Third Checkup: Fresh Manna, Fresh Manifestation

filled with is anything but the Lord. People who are filled with God and His presence can't help but talk about Jesus. I can tell what you are eating and digesting by listening to you talk for thirty minutes. If in thirty minutes, you don't somehow bring God into the conversation, then I know you aren't feeding on His Word and that there probably isn't much faith in you for fresh manna and fresh manifestations when they are needed. People who love fishing or football or classical music have a way of finding opportunities to insert their favorite hobbies into a conversation. It is so natural and so easy. The same should be true about Jesus. Is Jesus the first person you think about when you get up in the morning? Is He the last person you think about as you go to sleep? What is taking priority in your life? If not God, what can you do to begin to change the mental and spiritual environment in your own world?

You know what it is like to wake up in the morning or walk into your favorite restaurant and smell all of the fragrant aromas of the food that is to be served. So too with Jesus. We should anticipate some fresh and living bread being prepared for our walk with Him. Don't settle for the aromas of the world that will leave a putrefying foul odor clinging to your nostrils. Go after God and discover how good His fresh bread really is. That fresh bread or fresh manna will then set the tone for you to have and experience many fresh manifestations all through your day, and yes, even your life. It will be a pleasing testimony for you to enjoy all of your days.

Fourth Checkup
A Stone's Throw Away

I believe in doctors. Does that sound strange from a guy writing a book about supernatural healing? But it is true, and while my doctors are all believers, they don't all believe in supernatural healing, but most of them do; and that is okay. Jesus knew a doctor too, and his name was Luke. Luke wrote two books of the New Testament: Luke and Acts. Paul took Dr. Luke with him on many of the journeys recorded in the book of Acts, and I add that he did this because Paul was frequently getting beat up, and he needed a good doctor with him.

Over the years, my doctors have had me pray for them when they were sick or hurting, and some of them got well really quickly. We are all in this together, so we learn from each other, using the medical expertise and the supernatural knowledge from the Bible as well. With those thoughts in mind, let's dive into these next two stories and see what we can learn that make our exclamations of, "Well, well, well," just that much more meaningful.

I previously wrote in chapter two about my pain with IBS, but a recent experience eclipsed that three-year pain description and process in just seven days. That may seem extraordinarily strange, yet it is true. On May 8, 2014, after preaching and ministering at a midweek service at a local church in Omaha, I went home to discover a rather unusual and strong sudden pain in the lower right side of my back. I had just prayed for a man with similar symptoms, so I immediately thought that perhaps this was a demonic manifestation or attack because I have seen pain jump to others and to me while praying with people.

I have also seen pain move around a person's body when I am praying for a particular healing. When a symptom moves around while praying for someone else, that usually means there is a demonic presence trying to hide and not be identified. Not all sicknesses have a demonic presence, but many do. That is why in Acts 10:38 we are told that Jesus was anointed by the Holy Spirit and went about doing good and healing all who were oppressed by the devil.

So Diane and I began to intercede, and the pain subsided for a while but then actually got substantially worse. We read the Bible and prayed some more, and the pain again subsided, only to reoccur just a couple of hours later. I was about to do something that I had never done before in my life, and that was to go to the emergency room and check myself in for an examination. I had no idea what was happening at this point, so we called our son Jason at his nearby college, and he came to meet me at the ER. At midnight, when I arrived at the ER, there was, of course, a long waiting line, so I had to sit or lay in very uncomfortable positions for nearly an hour before I was seen by the ER staff.

The doctors and nurses thought it was most likely a kidney stone, and they ended up taking x-rays, giving me pain meds, and helping me relax for nearly six hours in the ER before I was released to go home. Eventually, the kidney stone was verified. The attending ER doctor was really nice and was a believer, and I had the opportunity to pray for him for about ten minutes too. It was a divine appointment in many ways. I went home on Friday morning and rested most of the day, and I really began to feel much better on Saturday too. But early Sunday morning, I had a recurring pain that was significant enough to warrant a return to the hospital.

Discovering Intercessors

During all of this, my son Jason and my wife Diane were really praying hard for me. I sometimes refer to my wife as my princess, but seeing her pray when I was in this much pain, I now refer to her as my warrior princess. Anyway, we went back to the ER in the early morning of Mother's Day and were there for another few hours until the pain significantly subsided. Once again, I prayed for some of the staff and witnessed to others.

Fourth Checkup: A Stone's Throw Away

Later that day, two good friends, Jerry and Melissa Kelly, came by to pray for me for an extended time in my home. This was followed by another friend, Fc Farwell, who also did the same. These three individuals served on my intercessory prayer team and have been a huge benefit to me in the area of prayer and ultimately teaching in our monthly seminars too. I am not sure I would have discovered them and their intercession gifts had I not been sick and going through this medical crisis.

Three days later, the pain came back, and I called a urologist and got an appointment. My wife drove me a long way to his office, but the pain was substantially worse than either of the two times I was in the ER, so they decided to admit me to a local hospital on that side of town. When we arrived, there was supposed to be a room waiting for me, but something happened that caused it to be unavailable, so I had more painful waiting, this time lying on the admitting room floor in utter agony.

Finally, I was admitted and had kidney stone removal surgery the next day. I was able to witness to many of the staff and pray with some of my nurses and other attendants—even the guy who took me to the surgery center and some of those in that center as well. I remember talking to them about the Lord. When I woke up in recovery, I was still talking, thinking that I was in the surgery center and not realizing that two hours had passed. I thought I was still talking to the surgery staff but soon realized that I was talking to the recovery nurse. The Lord gave me an opportunity to pray for her too, as she had ringing in her ears. She later sent me a note in the mail, thanking me for praying for her.

Prayerful Encouragement

When I checked out of the hospital later that day, the lady who took me to the driveway in the wheelchair stated she was sad to see me go. She told me that many of the staff were hoping that I would stay a couple of days. I was trying to figure this out and was kind of shocked, as I did not want to stay any longer. But she went on to tell me that I was the talk of the nurse's station. I asked why, and she said that I was one of the most positive and upbeat patients they had seen in a long time. They usually had complaining patients, but I had offered to pray for so many of them and gave so much encouragement that I was a joy to their lives and they just hoped I might stay around a few more days.

Even in the midst of a difficult situation, God used me to bring comfort, peace, prayer, and other ministry opportunities to those I was in contact with. God has a way of demonstrating His love for people, even in the midst of our own suffering and attempts to get well. It is not unusual for God to use our circumstances to propel His Kingdom forward if we will just be open to what he wants to do.

Now, please enjoy another kidney stone adventure from my friend Pastor Bill Wise. Pastor Bill is a retired Lutheran pastor now living in Florida. He also just spent a year at the Bethel School of Supernatural Ministry in Redding, California. His story is much different than mine, and God used him in different ways with different results and outcomes. It is a very unusual story, and I hope it ministers life and courage to you in any medical trials or other trials that you are currently walking through. I frequently tell people that if they are walking through hell, not to stop. Don't get a condo or a motel there; just keep going. We walk *through* stuff because we are going *to* something. The Bible says that the steps of righteous people are ordered by the Lord. So as you read this next testimony, keep that in mind and apply it to yourself as a possible answer for what you are currently experiencing.

A Reflection on Grace, Mercy, and Guidance

As the sun set in Poland on the last day of September, I reflected on how the Lord had blessed the ministry that week. Settling into bed, I thanked Jesus and looked forward to the trip into Slovakia the next morning. At 1:00 a.m., that all changed. I knew the sharp pain and pressure in my right kidney were telltale signs of a kidney stone. I had three previous kidney stones—one while in Nigeria

Fourth Checkup: A Stone's Throw Away

nearly a decade before. But I was not ready for what lay ahead.

I traveled to Bratislava and then to Piestany to meet with Jaroslav (Jerry) Duda. My battle with the stone continued with moderate pain. Midweek I visited the hospital in Levice, Slovakia, where an ultrasound and x-ray verified the situation: a very large stone that was refusing to budge more than halfway down the ureter. I was given a shot and an assortment of pain and anti-inflammatory meds and went on to Kosice for the weekend of ministry and preaching. Another trip to the hospital there provided little more insight, but another pain shot and further meds.

I was part of a two-man team leading half of a major seminar and conference of three hundred, involving many pastors and lay leaders from some fifty Lutheran churches around Slovakia. On Wednesday night, two days into the seminar, I was as miserable as I could be. Ten days of constant moderate-to-strong pain had taken its toll.

Choosing Options

I asked to be taken back to the Kosice hospital. They gave me another shot, reviewed the situation, discussed procedures and time frames, and then gave me three options: One was to be admitted, but they could not do surgery or lithotripsy (blasting) due to the stone's location. Perhaps in a week it would move, but by then I would miss my flight home. Option 2 was to return to the U.S. for treatment. Option 3 was to manage the pain through shots as needed.

I could get a flight home the next day and decided to take it. I knew this would be a major disappointment and problem for the conference, but the idea of facing pain for five more days was overwhelming. I had prayed so hard over the last week for God's deliverance and healing without seeing anything happen. I fell asleep at a pastor's house awaiting a 7 a.m. pickup for a 9 a.m. flight.

I was abruptly awakened at 4:30 a.m. with a terrifying thought: "My emotions, they are flat-lined. I am acting like a zombie." Then followed the concern for letting down the team and putting the tremendous pressure on the conference leaders—some of my friends. I called out to God, "Lord, I've got to hear from You. I haven't heard from You for more than a week—no Scripture, no impression, no answer!"

I was desperate. I told God, "You have got to speak to me! Give me a Bible passage from a book I seldom read and a chapter I probably have never read so I'll know it is You!" Ecclesiastes 8. That's what I saw in my mind. I lunged for my NIV Bible.

When God wants to get your attention, He gets it. Here is what I read:

8:1: "Who is like the **wise** man?" ...*Okay Lord, You've got my name and my attention (because my last name is "Wise").*

8:2: "Obey the king's command, I say, because you took an oath before God." *One thing I have consistently vowed is, "God, I'll go wherever You want me to go and do whatever You want me to do."*

Fourth Checkup: A Stone's Throw Away

8:3: "Do not be in a hurry to leave the king's presence." *Okay, you live in Slovakia too; I get the message!*

8:5–6: "Whoever obeys his command <u>will come to no harm</u>, and the wise heart will know the proper time and procedure. For there is a <u>proper time and procedure</u> for every matter, though a man's misery weighs heavily upon him." *Well, Lord, I guess You know my misery and my concern for kidney damage, and You have this thing planned out!*

8:8: "No one is discharged in time of war." ...*Okay, I get it!*

I changed the flight back to the original date of the fifteenth, called the team, and got a ride back to the conference. God provided here also, in that there was a doctor attending the conference who could get the pain shots in case I needed them.

But the Lord had more grace for me. He supernaturally kept my pain and nausea at a low level for the remaining four days in Slovakia so I could concentrate on the ministry. The teaching sessions went fine, but probably the greater impact was illustrated by several emails I received upon returning home.

One wrote, "Both you and Doug were a blessing for us at the Conference and seminar! It was great to be a part of the team with both of you! I think you were an example of faith for many of us also when dealing with pain and coming back from the hospital with the Lord's word of encouragement."

Another wrote, "Your forbearance and courageousness was for me a shining example."

What God Taught Me

It's not about me, but about Him.
It's not about me, but about them.
It's not about then, but about now.
It's not about doing, but about being.
It's not about feelings; it's about faithfulness.
It's not about complaining, but about listening.
It's about His grace, mercy, power, and guidance.

"My grace is sufficient for you, for my power is made perfect in weakness" (2 Corinthians 12:9).

Epilogue

I returned home on October 15, saw a urologist, had CT scan, and was scheduled for surgery on October 25. But God intervened on the 24th, and I passed the stone. Isn't God good?!

Recognition vs. Competition

Let me add the Scriptural premise for my first book, *Downloads from Heaven*, in which I used and often quoted John 5:19. Jesus stated that He only did what He saw the father doing. For Pastor Bill, he chose to remain overseas and persevere through the ordeal. That may not be the case for everyone. I know in my past there were a few times when I probably should have gone to the ER, but through prayer (and probably just plain stubbornness), I elected not to go; but this particular time, I did. There is nothing wrong with either his choice or mine.

I operate on a principle of recognition, not competition. We do not respond based on what someone else has done or is experiencing, but on what we sense the Lord would have us do in

Fourth Checkup: A Stone's Throw Away

each of those situations. Sometimes in public I pray for people, and sometimes I don't. Occasionally in church I lay my hands on people for healing, and sometimes I don't. There are times I quote Scriptures, and there are times I don't. I try really hard just to do what I see my Lord doing, and then do that with Him. I am a coworker and co-laborer with Him, so I am embracing what He is doing, not what He is not doing.

Obviously, God heals through doctors, and He also heals supernaturally. I am okay with both and recognize that it is His deal, His plan, and His will, so that keeps me positioned to walk in humility and see Him get the glory, while occasionally, I get the hugs. Regardless of how someone gets well or healed, it is so much fun to declare when it is completed, "Well, well, well!"

Fifth Checkup
Aye Aye—Eye Eye!

While Diane and I were driving in Council Bluffs, Iowa, we noticed a pickup truck that was full of corn on the side of the road, so we pulled in to check the prices and see the produce. I pulled up near the back of the truck and let the engine of my SUV keep running while I stepped out of the vehicle and engaged the older gentleman in conversation. Diane remained in the SUV while I asked the man how much his corn was. I then asked him where it came from, and he told me it was from his farm and that he has 1700 acres of corn in Shenandoah, Iowa.

I asked him why he was selling corn on the side of the road in Council Bluffs if he had a farm that large, and he responded that his wife asked him the same question. His answer was that he enjoyed meeting interesting people just like me. His price was reasonable, so I told him I would take a dozen ears. Our conversation continued, and I learned that he has been married for sixty-two years, that he got married right out of high school, and that he was now eighty years old.

At this point, I decided to share that while he liked to meet people, I enjoyed praying with folks. Then I added a couple of prayer testimonies and asked him if he needed prayer, to which he said he did not. I asked him if he was in pain, but he said, "No." I inquired about a couple of other possible prayer needs, to which I received the same answer of "No."

I then asked him if he liked to read, and he stated that he could not read. I knew he had graduated from high school, so I asked him why he could not read. He pointed to his body and said there was a gland inside that was malfunctioning and that both of his eyes were lazy and would not focus to read properly. I gave two really cool testimonies of healing, including one of a local friend who had been deaf for twenty-eight years but was healed supernaturally when I prayed for him. Then I offered to pray for this man selling corn, and this time, he said, "Yes!"

The distance between us was about three feet as I prayed a thirty-second prayer, speaking healing, asking for a healing anointing, and praying for recovery of his eyesight and a creative miracle for this gland that was not functioning properly. When I concluded, I stated that there is a miracle when you check and asked if he could tell if there was any improvement. He immediately said things looked clearer and brighter. So I grabbed one of my books out of the car, opened it to a smaller paragraph, and asked him to read it. With his fingers pointing at the words, he read it at a normal pace without any problems, and he was genuinely surprised and elated. He let me know that normally he reads very, very slowly, pronouncing each word with all of the syllables and taking a sentence or paragraph extremely slowly, but he was able to read this with ease and without any difficulty.

Then he startled me and said, "Wait a minute!" I honestly did not expect what was coming, but then he told me with an excited voice that he had just read that paragraph without his glasses on, as he had forgotten to bring them with him. He told me that he normally reads slowly and always with his glasses on, but now he had just read at a normal pace and without his glasses.

I offered him my book and suggested he read it and send me an email as to how he liked it, but he told me that he doesn't do email or computers at all, because the print is too small and he can't read. But then I told him, "Well, you can read now," and he responded, "Yes, I can," shook my hand with a firm grip, took my book, and said, "God Bless you." Now that is an effective story with lots of energy.

Proverbs 23:12 says, "Apply your heart to instruction and your ears to words of knowledge." Those are not corn ears, but your personal ears. We need to be instructed and apply understanding and knowledge so that we can be more effective.

Fifth Checkup: Aye Aye—Eye Eye!

Believing Is Seeing

Most of us have read and understand Hebrews 11:1, which says, "Now faith is the substance of things hoped for, the evidence of things not seen." Many people want to see what God is doing first and then respond, but His way of doing things is to ask us to respond in faith by believing first and then seeing the results.

In the movie *The Santa Claus 2*, Charlie says, "Seeing isn't believing; believing is seeing."[3] While this is a secular movie, the point of the quote is genuine and authentic when it comes to Christianity and our walk as disciples of Jesus, Who asks us to lay down what we can see and follow Him—not blindly, but in faith to that which is not seen.

Here is another way of looking at this in James 5:16–18:

> Confess your trespasses to one another, and pray for one another, that you may be healed. The effective, fervent prayer of a righteous man avails much. Elijah was a man with a nature like ours, and he prayed earnestly that it would not rain; and it did not rain on the land for three years and six months. And he prayed again, and the heaven gave rain, and the earth produced its fruit.

We will study this passage more in depth in the next chapter, but notice the phrase that depicts Elijah was a man.

As I stated in a previous chapter, my wife has become a warrior princess when it comes to prayer. She is normally very quiet and reserved, peaceful and calm, but when the enemy is attacking and our norm is disrupted by ungodly influence, she has become and is very effective in prayer, and I am grateful.

John Wesley once stated that God does nothing on earth unless someone prays. I once countered with this additional thought: God won't answer something in prayer that is not asked. Do you think that is true? It actually isn't, because in Ephesians 3:20 we learn that God is able to do exceedingly and abundantly above and beyond all that we can ask or think. So, what is my point? We need to learn what is true and what is not true when it comes to prayer, rather than responding, "Well, well, well, I guess God did not want to do that or answer that prayer." We need to know what the Bible says about prayer and how we can apply instruction and words of knowledge from His world to ours.

I believe that Jesus went from one prayer meeting to another and did ministry in-between. In other words, Jesus was a man of prayer, seeking information, instruction, and guidance from His Father so that He knew how to respond, what to do, and what not to do in every situation. He even stated in John 5:30 that He could not do anything of Himself, and that He only did the will of the Father who sent Him. This is an understanding that we need to apply and grasp. It is time we quit blaming our personal failures in prayer on the will of God when we don't really know the will of God.

Power to Heal

In Matthew 10:8 we are told to heal the sick. So when I came across a man selling corn, I did not ask God to heal him, but instead I spoke healing, confessed it, and believed it as being true from Matthew 10:8. Recently, I was at a family's home, sharing about this and teaching them about declaring healing rather than asking for it. After thirty minutes of teaching, I asked them if they were ready to pray for the person in the room who was sick, and they said they understood the principles and then began to ask and actually plead with God, almost begging the Lord to touch this person. I stopped them and asked what they were doing, in light of everything I just shared, and they said they felt like they would be demanding of God and could not do that.

We were in the kitchen at the time, and I pointed to the appliances on the counter and stated that each one of them relied on electricity to function, but if the appliances were not connected to the plugs in the wall and not accessing the power in the walls, they would not work. I then shared that in order for any electrical appliance to function, it must have direct access to the power.

Fifth Checkup: Aye Aye—Eye Eye!

Behind every electrical plug is a circuit carrying electrical power. The power is there, but if we don't put a demand on it, the appliance won't work. The electrical power in our house belongs to us because we pay for it to be there. In the same way, we can also put a demand on the power of God. This power belongs to us because God has paid for it and has freely given us access to it. As previously stated, we have the run of the house!

In Luke 9:1–2 we are told that we have been given power and authority. Power is the strength and might to complete a task, but authority is the right to use that power. When I pray for others, I want access to that power because I want to be effective and full of godly energy to complete the task. Bill Johnson has stated that power is the ability to ride a wave, but authority is the right to create a wave. I want and have access to both, and I don't have to plead and beg and create a scene, but rather just almost nonchalantly plug into the power and put a demand on it, and people get well. It is that simple.

Miracles and Doctors

Of course, at this point you are probably asking about the previous chapters dealing with doctors and surgery and other means of healing, and I won't avoid this topic, but just respond by stating that I am in favor of healing and so is Jesus. Jesus selected a doctor to be a part of His ongoing staff, so I believe that Jesus, along with many others, agreed that all healing comes from God, whether at the hands of a skilled surgeon, a gifted and caring nurse, an educated specialist, or an anointed man or woman of God used in prayer to see healing displayed. It is not either-or, but rather both-and; all that combines for a well-rounded and balanced approach to biblical healing.

I wear glasses, and that requires a prescription after an examination from an eye specialist, yet I have prayed for and seen many eye miracles and supernatural healings, such as those healed from crossed eyes, blurred vision, tunnel vision, glaucoma, macular degeneration, partial blindness, and many others. The testimony at the beginning of this chapter is one such eye miracle.

A story in the Bible is recorded of Jesus actually praying for a blind man two times. There are many reasons given by numerous theologians and students of the Bible for this passage, but the clear answer to me is that Jesus knew what He was doing, and He was following the instructions of His Father, which is what we are to do too. If God says to go to the doctor, we should respond. If He says go forward for prayer, then that should be our response. Paul told Timothy to drink some wine for his stomach ailment. Since this is written in Scripture, I believe that Paul was inspired by the Holy Spirit to share this information with Timothy.

I remember praying for a lady in Des Moines, Iowa, who could hardly read the big "E" on the eye chart, and the lines under it were often fuzzy. But after about ten minutes of prayer, she could read font size fourteen easily and read portions of her Bible to the church family there. It was a wonderful blessing to see (no pun intended).

Obedience is Key

My friend Sam Hinn (who wrote an endorsement for this book) posted this on Facebook one day, and he granted me permission to share it in my book, so here it is for you to consider:

> The success of your tomorrow is in direct proportion to the depth of your obedience today. Every act of obedience is an investment in your future. Acts of obedience have the power to position or reposition us for greater abundance of God. When we are obedient, a chain of events will come together, and like the pieces of a puzzle, they create a picture of God's goodness in our lives. We must stop thinking about the COST of obedience and consider the PRICE of disobedience!
>
> Disobedience is the cancer that eats away at our hopes and dreams, destroying any chance of success in the future. The bottom line is that our future and

Fifth Checkup: Aye Aye—Eye Eye!

destiny are shaped by our acts of obedience or our acts of disobedience. Like it or not, the things we reap are often the consequences of our own actions. Peter's obedience enabled him to catch a net full of fish, and because of Jonah's disobedience, the fish caught him. Every major promotion comes from personal obedience, not performance.

Let me add in Isaiah 1:19, which declares, "If you are willing and obedient,
You shall eat the good of the land." I have quoted this verse many times and frequently with this emphasis: Most believers in God are willing, but many do not get to the obedience stage; and then there are those who are obedient, but they do it unwillingly with an attitude of: *I will do this, but I don't want to, and I don't expect much to happen either.*

So what does it boil down to? We are to be obedient, much like a good soldier (highlighted in 2 Timothy 2) who carries out his or her assignment from those who are higher in rank than he or she is. In the military, the response is always with a salute and the words, "Yes, sir" or "Yes, ma'am." In the navy, I believe they say, "Aye Aye!"

From the Urban Dictionary we discover a more in-depth meaning to this term: "Naval response indicating that an order has been received, is understood, and will be carried out immediately. In operational situations, this is usually shortened to simply 'aye.' In contrast to 'Aye Aye sir,' a response of 'Yes Sir' usually indicates that the person understands but is contemplating performing the ordered task at a later time or date."[4]

Of course, I used the term as a play on words for the title of this chapter dealing with eye healings, but the significance is clear, as depicted in Proverbs 16:12–14: "A worthless person, a wicked man, walks with a perverse mouth; he winks with his eyes, he shuffles his feet, he points with his fingers; perversity is in his heart, he devises evil continually, he sows discord." A wink is a form of teasing, with a portion of unbelief tied to it; plus, a wink is an eye movement with a shadow of darkness attached to it. Even the tiniest of darkness is not to be tolerated for those who walk in the light of Jesus.

So a wink implies an attitude that you are not fully committed to the process, but with the salute and the words, "Yes, Sir," or "Aye Aye," we see a significant hand-to-eye coordination that includes strict obedience and observation of what the order is that is to be carried out. Jesus prayed for six different blind folks six different ways. His attitude was that He was to do what He saw the Father doing (John 5:19). That must be our response, as well. Otherwise, what we end up with is something far short of what God really intended to happen.

Ephesians 6:5–7 records it this way: "Bondservants, be obedient to those who are your masters according to the flesh, with fear and trembling, in sincerity of heart, as to Christ; not with eye-service, as men-pleasers, but as bondservants of Christ, doing the will of God from the heart, with goodwill doing service, as to the Lord, and not to men." A wink includes the thought of eye-service but without a deep commitment to the process and the response that God is asking of us.

Trust me when I say that God often has me pray for people for healing in radically different ways. In a healing service, you may often hear me say something like this: "I have never done or said this before." I am not motivated by methods and previous ways of seeing the miraculous accomplished; rather, I really do try to focus and center on what God is saying to any particular situation.

Once, while I was preaching on the subject of "Fresh Manna, Fresh Manifestation" to a large conference of about a thousand people, God had told me in advance that at some point I would be praying for eye problems in the middle of the message. And sure enough, about one third of the way into the message, He had me stop and identify anyone with eye problems, including floaters, shooting stars, shadows, and other blockages in the eyes.

So I asked everyone to stand who had these symptoms and to lay their own hands on their eyes right where they stood in their rows while I offered a simple prayer for healing. After this brief prayer, I asked for a show of hands from those who had definite

Fifth Checkup: Aye Aye—Eye Eye!

improvement, and over fifty people raised their hands. Later, and throughout the conference, I had a number of people come up to me and share that their eyes were still well and healed, including a pastor who repeatedly told me that as a teenager she had been in some sort of accident that left a zigzag shadow in one eye that looked like a lightning bolt to her, but that after I had prayed, this pattern had vanished from her eyes, and her eyes were now clear for the first time in forty or more years. I did not even pray for that specific eye problem, but God knew. I was obedient to stop the message and pray, and those who wanted healing were obedient to stand up, even though it was not an official prayer time at the conclusion of a message.

You see, we often get religious and think we have to do it a certain way at a definite time with a certain pattern to get the results; but God knows, and if we just follow Him, then He says in Psalm 32:8 that He will guide us with His eye. What better option is there than this? When you can see someone's eye, you know you have to be pretty close to see it, so our proximity to Jesus is very important too.

One of my favorite verses is from 2 Chronicles 16:9: "For the eyes of the LORD run to and fro throughout the whole earth, to show Himself strong on behalf of those whose heart is loyal to Him." God is using His eyes to look for someone like you and me who is simply loyal. The verse does not say we have to be perfect, but just loyal. That is a wonderful blessing.

Let's just add in Ephesians 1:17–19 as we conclude this chapter: "That the God of our Lord Jesus Christ, the Father of glory, may give to you the spirit of wisdom and revelation in the knowledge of Him, the eyes of your understanding being enlightened; that you may know what is the hope of His calling, what are the riches of the glory of His inheritance in the saints, and what is the exceeding greatness of His power toward us who believe, according to the working of His mighty power." Since God tells us that He will guide us with His eye, I honestly believe that He never winks or blinks, but rather keeps His eyes open and focused on us.

This song by Paul Baloche really depicts a great desire that is worth sharing as we transition from this chapter to the next. If you know it, go ahead and sing it rather than just reading the words. Go ahead; I know you want to. I believe I can see you doing that right now.

"Open the Eyes of My Heart"[5]

Open the eyes of my heart, Lord
Open the eyes of my heart
I want to see You
I want to see You

To see You high and lifted up
Shining in the light of Your glory
Pour out Your power and love
As we sing holy, holy, holy

Holy, holy, holy
Holy, holy, holy
Holy, holy, holy
I want to see you

Sixth Checkup
Effective Energy

As I shared in the previous chapter, I am now going to discuss and teach further about the passage in James 5:16–18, which will hopefully bring a clearer vision to what God was saying when the Holy Spirit inspired James to compose this section of the Bible.

> Confess your trespasses to one another, and pray for one another, that you may be healed. The effective, fervent prayer of a righteous man avails much. Elijah was a man with a nature like ours, and he prayed earnestly that it would not rain; and it did not rain on the land for three years and six months. And he prayed again, and the heaven gave rain, and the earth produced its fruit.

An effective, fervent prayer makes a way for God to act and respond. We have many choices in life and in our walks with God, and one of the choices with the Lord is whether to be efficient or effective, and then whether to be affective or effective.

Let's start with the second one first. To be *affective* means to touch a heart, but to be *effective* means to change a heart. As my heart is changed, I can then help change the lives of others through godly, inspired, anointed discipleship that Jesus called us to participate in. Often, believers have their hearts and lives touched by God, but is there lasting change? I'm not sure, as many return to the same patterns, habits, and addictions right after receiving the deliverance, healing, or provision that they were seeking. I know I have been guilty of this myself in years past, but I am working hard to discover how to maintain and keep the fire burning bright long after the prayer has been answered.

Efficient or Effective?

Now let's proceed and look at the difference between being efficient and effective. In Luke 10:38–42, Dr. Luke reveals an interesting story about two sisters who happen to have welcomed Jesus into their house. We are told that Martha was busy serving and in fact was efficient, or doing things right. And who would argue against hospitality and preparations, especially when hosting a guest in your house? But Jesus let all of us know that Mary was more effective because she had chosen to do the right thing. Doing things right or doing the right thing: You decide. Jesus tried to help Martha understand that, in essence, she was preparing sandwiches and soup that He had never asked for. Mary, on the other hand, was much more effective because she had chosen simply to sit by His feet, listen, and be filled with spiritual food, rather than preparing natural food that would only satisfy for a short period of time.

The word *effective*, used in James 5, literally means to be active in or engaged in something that produces superhuman responses and action, with divine energy. It comes from the Greek word *energeo*, which depicts powerful and lasting energy. Martha's energy level would soon wear out due to her wearisome serving, but Mary's would be propelled to the next level as a result of just spending quality time in the presence of Jesus. If you were to use this effective word in a military context, it would be like comparing someone who is in active duty to someone who is enjoying military retirement. When on active duty, you can be called up at a moment's notice and deployed to wherever the military wants to send you.

Now let's look at three other places this word *effective* is used to help us discern its use and receive revelation on how the energy from being effective brings increased value to our lives as we walk in Kingdom authority, revelation, and purpose. The first one is in Ephesians 4:16, which comes after the discourse of the five-fold ministry being given in verse eleven and some of the benefits of those ministries being modeled and followed by others who love Jesus: "From whom the whole body, joined and knit

Sixth Checkup: Effective Energy

together by what every joint supplies, according to the effective working by which every part does its share, causes growth of the body for the edifying of itself in love."

The effective working of the body in love produces godly energy that promotes encouragement, preparation, and sustaining life in the early church and today, if put into practice. It is not just some religious formula, but rather a pattern that Paul is sharing that promotes and propels the church to new heights and better enablement as they function in this sphere of energy that God provides. It's kind of like God commanding the blessing where there is unity (Psalm 133). He releases energy where there is cohesiveness, brotherly authenticity, and when everyone works together. We could almost respond, "Well, well, well—I knew there must be something to these verses in Ephesians that I never saw before, and now I know."

Paul previously declared this truth in Ephesians 3:7: "Of which I became a minister according to the gift of the grace of God given to me by the effective working of His power." The phrase *working of His power* is actually the same as the word *effective*, so there is a double emphasis added to this call, where the ministry of Paul is like a double portion of energy being drawn out of Paul as he ministered and then shared with those who received the ministry.

And then Ephesians 1:19 adds more dimensions to this particular brand of energy: "And what is the exceeding greatness of His power toward us who believe, according to the working of His mighty power." And while the word *effective* is not actually used here in this passage, the same meaning is displayed behind the two places that power is used in the passage. There is a greatness to His power and a working of His mighty power released through belief that it will indeed happen. Faith is the kicker that sends this game into overtime for a sudden-death playoff, in which the enemy loses and the King of Kings is crowned as the Victor. We who believe also share in that victory, as if we were on the same field at the very same moment.

Righteousness Revealed

But there is another element in the James passage that must be addressed, even if briefly, and that is the word *righteous*. The effective, fervent prayer of a righteous person avails much or accomplishes much. Being righteous is not something we do, but rather someone we are. We are the righteousness of God in Christ Jesus. Jesus became sin, and we became righteous, and there was a great exchange that took place, putting us in new positions for greater effectiveness. Yes, I am using the word in the definition to express and convey the total commitment that Jesus has to this process. We don't become righteous on our own by something that we do, but we become righteous with Jesus because of something he already did. Being in that state of righteousness, coupled with effectiveness, releases power that no devil in hell can touch, erase, or destroy. When people know who they are in Jesus, they are indeed formidable foes against the enemies of the cross and against the adversaries of the Kingdom of God.

Being effective with energy is then met with righteousness that projects a power surge into the prayer room. Life as we know it changes in a moment because of the fusion of these two spiritual dynamics working together in harmony and unity. Many believers are somewhat effective but lack that extra bounce or shockwave of anointed current because they don't walk in or understand the righteousness aspect.

Let me explain with this verse. Isaiah 54:17 imparts this vision to us: "'No weapon formed against you shall prosper, and every tongue which rises against you in judgment You shall condemn. This is the heritage of the servants of the LORD, and their righteousness is from Me,' says the LORD."

Most believers love the first part of this verse that no weapon formed against them shall prosper. Wow, what a promise, and what a declaration! This is fantastic. And many also love the part about other people not judging you or having a critical spirit about them. We often jump to these verses and want the freedom and opportunity to be free from attacks but then decline to accept the second part of the verse that declares that our righteousness is from the Lord. For some reason, some people just don't want to receive or agree that their righteousness is from God, but rather want to work at it over and over until they get to a point where they have somehow earned it. None of the attributes or promises in this verse are earned. All of them come as result of having a relationship with the God of the universe because He loves us and freely offers us these things as a part of being adopted into His family. This Scripture clearly says that this is the heritage of the servants of the Lord. We have a heritage that is ours simply because we serve Jesus, and being righteous is one of many parts that are included.

But I want to address why so many will accept the first two blessings of this verse but want to eliminate the righteousness portion. That is because of things in the past that they have not been able to get beyond. It is because their memory of certain non-righteous elements and obstacles that have been long forgiven by God are still remembered in their non-forgiven state by the individuals. Many people are more unforgiving of themselves than God ever is. Often believers find it difficult to appropriate God's forgiveness. They often feel that they have to go a certain period of time without being involved in that particular sin in order for God to forgive them. It is these obstacles that often prevent the right attitude of righteousness from being revealed, manifested, and freely embraced just as true and just as easily as the option of "no weapon that is formed shall prosper."

Living Beyond

Charles Swindoll wrote a two-volume book set that he titled *Living Beyond the Daily Grind*. His goal was to equip the readers with teachings that would help eliminate those things that steal our joy in our daily walks with Jesus, providing we actually do have <u>*daily*</u> walks.

Among the major "thieves" that steal our joy and upset our day-to-day activities are sins that keep surfacing from our past, which normally, when analyzed, are brought up by our own selves in our own thought lives, thus disrupting our forward progress with negative thoughts of the past. These sometimes come in waves of persistent problems that try to knock us off our feet so that we collapse and lose the ground that we have gained through intentional disciple training. The enemy likes to use these tactics to destroy our faith and get us doubting that God really cares for us. Just like a surfer when he gets knocked off his board and paddles out to catch another wave, so should we as believers get back up and face our adversary with the power of God's Word.

Paul addresses this problem in Philippians 3:12–15:

> Not that I have already attained, or am already perfected; but I press on, that I may lay hold of that for which Christ Jesus has also laid hold of me. Brethren, I do not count myself to have apprehended; but one thing I do, forgetting those things which are behind and reaching forward to those things which are ahead, I press toward the goal for the prize of the upward call of God in Christ Jesus.
>
> Therefore let us, as many as are mature, have this mind; and if in anything you think otherwise, God will reveal even this to you.

Please notice that Paul gives instructions on a one-step motion that, if followed, will eliminate many of the problems you face today. He says, "But one thing I do." One thing! One thing! Just one thing. One thing is not too much to take on at once, is it? It sounds easy and manageable, and it is. But look at it a bit closer. Paul goes on to illustrate what this one thing is, and if you read it closely, you will think that it is actually three things and that there is a mistake in the Bible.

He says that, forgetting those things that are behind and reaching forward to those things ahead, he then pressed toward the goal. Yes, that sounds like three things, and if tackled alone, most people will never get past the first one. But it is all one motion

Sixth Checkup: Effective Energy

with God. Forgetting the past, reaching forward, and pressing in for more, is all one motion. It's one swing of the bat, with a step into the swing and the follow-through as well. It is aiming the bowling ball, walking past the arrows in the lane, moving your arm back to swing that ball forward, and propelling it down the center alley for a strike.

This is predicated on the previous verses where Paul stated that he is conformed to the death of Jesus. Dead men don't have a past that they talk about. After death the only observation is what lies ahead, and that choice was made before the grave. Jesus does not send anyone to heaven, nor does He send them to hell. The choice to follow Jesus and enjoy the finished work on the cross is for those who love the Lord in life now and in the life to come. If we have died to ourselves and are embracing the Cross, we need to stop talking about the past as if it controls our present and future times. Dead men don't feel pain.

Maturity Is a Sign

But there is one more aspect about this section from Philippians 3 that I want you to notice, and that is in verse fifteen. Paul states that those who are mature will have this same mind, same thought pattern, and same conviction. Maturity is measured on how you are able to forget the past, and with one motion, reach forward, while simultaneously pressing into the Kingdom of God for more. It is only an immature believer that wallows in his pity parties, reflecting on all the bad things that have happened, whether self-induced or slammed against you by others like a body check in ice hockey.

We often feel compelled to linger in the past just long enough to give us an excuse as to why God can't use us and why He would want to use someone else who perhaps is more qualified without such a sordid past, so as to give an excuse that makes sense to that person. But in reality, it is a lame excuse, and God came to deliver the lame and help them walk again.

"Yesterday is gone. Tomorrow has not yet come. We have only today. Let us begin" (Mother Teresa). Rick Warren said that we are products of our past, but we don't have to be prisoners of it. And Oscar Wilde said that no man is rich enough to buy back his past. There is a reason why your car's windshield is so much larger than the rear view mirror. Think about that for a moment!

It is very important that you don't let your past have a stranglehold on your life that squeezes the future life and breath out of you, while you gasp and struggle with past thoughts, actions and activities. Your past will often discourage you, thus providing avenues to remain discouraged in your present life too and never really look forward with any encouragement because of this frozen state of mummified existence, trying to preserve a past that is not worth preserving. Do not be a member of the frozen chosen.

Paul is basically saying, "Do not let your past trap you from running free in the present and future life that God has planned for you." Only immature people would intentionally step into a trap that is designed to snap shut and keep their legs immoveable while they hang upside-down, trying to free themselves from this self-inflicted trap of a previous time.

And then the real challenge comes when you want to step out and pray for someone, and your past jumps into your eyes and you chicken out because you have not learned how to appropriate and put on the righteous robe that God has ironed, pressed, and cleaned for you to wear. It is magnified if you're praying for deliverance or protection from some sin issue that got you down years ago; but now you are praying for someone else with similar tactical problems and issues, and the enemy whispers in your ear, "Remember when you used to do this? Who are you to now pray for someone else to get deliverance when it took you so long to get free?"

Freedom Encounter

Whether praying for yourself or someone else, don't let the past dictate your response to the Lord's future direction. View His strategy as one that describes a mature believer who is forgetting the past, while reaching forward, and pressing in as one big motion. This helps get rid of previous emotions and failures, while

Sixth Checkup: Effective Energy

setting you on a journey that has you proclaiming, "Well, well, well, just look what the Lord has done!"

With this anointed and effective energy, you will soon be soaring above your past and helping others to do the same. Simultaneously, you will be projecting life and godliness on others who are trying to move onward and upward. This then becomes a joy, without any hindrance of the past sneaking in and playing hide and seek in your heart. With previous entrenched darkness removed, you can then share the light with others that you now enjoy as a byproduct of knowing Jesus.

That phrase in Isaiah 54:17 about condemning any tongue that rises up against you might just imply that you have to condemn your own tongue and cheerfully say, "No, that is behind me, and it's forgiven and forgotten. I am not going to bring it up, and I am not going to let those thoughts condemn me. I am free in Christ Jesus, and as a mature believer, I intend to stay that way." Romans 8:1 tells us that there is no condemnation for those who are in Christ Jesus. If you are experiencing any condemnation, it is not coming from the Lord. So either the enemy is bringing it up to control you and thwart your Kingdom projections, or your own mind is betraying you with a lie; and when we agree with a lie, we empower the liar. It is time to empower the Word and let the Word empower you. That's what a Kingdom Encounter is all about.

There have been a number of times when I was trying to pray for someone for supernatural healing or deliverance, and only when dealing with the past and helping the person also deal with the past did the breakthrough come for them in the present. We must be sensitive to people's history but also help them see the value of reaching forward rather than backward to then eliminate the problem at hand. Sometimes, only in breaking yokes of bondages to the past or coming against family strongholds is the supernatural provision, healing, and miraculous power of God then able to bring the needed breakthrough.

These are times when you must hear from God with pinpoint accuracy and help the person get free and then not be entangled again with the yoke of bondage, just like Galatians 5:1 proposes: "Stand fast in the liberty by which Christ has set us free, and do not be entangled again in the yoke of bondage." Please notice the word *again*. *Again* implies a release from bondage while building on something positive in the realm of freedom. John 8:32 adds, "And you shall know the truth and the truth shall set you free." Stay free!

Seventh Checkup
EE2

In this chapter we will continue on with the theme of Effective Energy (hence, EE2), by launching with this true story. In 2010 around Thanksgiving, the college football bowl invitations were being announced, and the Nebraska Cornhuskers were invited to participate in the Holiday Bowl in San Diego.

We follow the Huskers because we live in Nebraska, but we also root for and follow the Wisconsin Badgers because Diane is from Wisconsin, USC because I am from Southern California, and the University of Texas because Jason was born in Texas. More recently, we have added in the Oklahoma Sooners and also Kansas State due to personal reasons that I am not going to share presently, but our hope and goal is that surely one of these teams can win a national championship!

Rain, Rain, Huskers Win Anyway

Anyway, since I am from San Diego (which is where the Holiday Bowl is played) and I had enough airline miles to take my family, I thought it would be cool to go to San Diego and watch the game. After all, I know how to navigate around the city and my brother, who wrote part of the First Checkup, has a condo near the beach that he will let me use for a family rate, so all I would have to pay for is a rental car, food, and the game tickets.

So I just prayed and asked God about it, and He immediately told me it was going to rain. Now there are times when God tells me the weather patterns and lets me pray to change them, but this was not one of those times. He expressly told me it was going to rain and rain hard, and the choice was ours as to whether (and weather) we wanted to attend or not. I shared this with my family and prayed some more, and every time I prayed I heard it was going to rain.

I checked on the Internet about the Holiday Bowl history, and in the previous thirty bowl games, it had never rained. December is not normally the rainy season in California. That is one reason the Rose Parade on January 1 is generally rain-free too. But again, each time I prayed, I heard it was going to rain, so we decided about five weeks in advance of the game not to go because God said it was going to rain.

And boy, did it ever rain! It rained so hard that the stadium parking lot and even the field were flooded a couple days in advance of the game, and the night of the game it rained the entire time. Nebraska easily beat Arizona that night, and in fact, Arizona did not score a point. I suspect that Arizona just is not that familiar with rain anyhow, but the point is that God spoke to us several weeks in advance and shared with us the weather forecast, and that is the only year in the history of the Holiday Bowl that it has ever rained.

So here is that energized effective Scripture from James 5:16–18 for you to read once again.

> Confess your trespasses to one another, and pray for one another, that you may be healed. The effective, fervent prayer of a righteous man avails much. Elijah was a man with a nature like ours, and he prayed earnestly that it would not rain; and it did not rain on the land for three years and six months. And he prayed again, and the heaven gave rain, and the earth produced its fruit.

As I write this chapter, it is my thirty-fifth wedding anniversary with Diane, and we posted some pictures on Facebook from early in our marriage. On our tenth anniversary year, we decided we wanted to return to Lake Tahoe during the Christmas season, as we were going to celebrate our engagement that happened there as well. As we were flying, the pilot came on and said that a snow storm was moving air traffic to Las Vegas and that would be our new destination for Christmas. This was substantially less than ideal. If you live in Vegas, please understand that our goal was to get to Lake Tahoe filled with natural beauty and wonder, not to be in a wall-to-wall city of hotels and casinos.

Diane and I began to pray, and we prayed, and we prayed—sometimes in English and sometimes in the Spirit—but with lots of energy; and suddenly, the pilot came on the speaker again and said, "Well, folks, for some reason the storm seems to be moving away from Reno, so we are going there after all." We landed safely in Reno, rented our car, and drove over the pass in the mountains to Lake Tahoe, and then it began to snow and snow and snow and snow. It snowed twenty-four inches in twelve hours. That is a lot! And Lake Tahoe was empty, so to speak, on Christmas Eve and Day, as many others could not drive in there. But we had the favor of God and the okay to pray for the weather to be changed.

Elijah the Man

In 1 Kings 17 we see how this story unfolds that is summarized in James 5 and compared in teaching to prayer:

> And Elijah the Tishbite, of the inhabitants of Gilead, said to Ahab, "As the LORD God of Israel lives, before whom I stand, there shall not be dew nor rain these years, except at my word."
>
> Then the word of the LORD came to him, saying, "Get away from here and turn eastward, and hide by the Brook Cherith, which flows into the Jordan. And it will be that you shall drink from the brook, and I have commanded the ravens to feed you there."
>
> So he went and did according to the word of the LORD, for he went and stayed by the Brook Cherith, which flows into the Jordan. The ravens brought him bread and meat in the morning, and bread and meat in the evening; and he drank from the brook.

And it happened after a while that the brook dried up, because there had been no rain in the land.

And if you kept reading in 1 Kings 17 you would see story after story of provision for Elijah and also for those that he was near or staying with. God takes care of Elijah after he delivers the word of God about the weather and then continues to provide during the drought. It is a story full of energy, fulfillment, and heavenly provision.

From 1 Kings 18 we read the end of the story:

Then Elijah said to Ahab, "Go up, eat and drink; for there is the sound of abundance of rain." So Ahab went up to eat and drink. And Elijah went up to the top of Carmel; then he bowed down on the ground, and put his face between his knees, and said to his servant, "Go up now, look toward the sea."

So he went up and looked, and said, "There is nothing." And seven times he said, "Go again."

Then it came to pass the seventh time, that he said, "There is a cloud, as small as a man's hand, rising out of the sea!" So he said, "Go up, say to Ahab, 'Prepare your chariot, and go down before the rain stops you.'"

Now it happened in the meantime that the sky became black with clouds and wind, and there was a heavy rain. So Ahab rode away and went to Jezreel. Then the hand of the LORD came upon Elijah; and he girded up his loins and ran ahead of Ahab to the entrance of Jezreel.

Let me tell you that if you can outrun a chariot you obviously are full of anointed effective energy. All through the story, God is providing and Elijah is staying active. He was not complaining about his situation or the fact that birds were bringing him food or that he had to stay with a widow with just a bit of flour and oil. Elijah was active in each situation, following the Lord's directions and plans and working the ministry that he was given.

In James 5 we are told that Elijah was a man—not a great prophet or an anointed television evangelist or the pastor of the largest church in town—just a man who liked to hang out with God and be used by God. And so it is with you and me, as we are just people wanting to be with the Lord, and we don't have to have a special title or calling to be used by God. All we need is the radical obedience that I wrote about in the last chapter and a willingness to move on with God. And this happens through faith as we trust God and then use our faith to follow His directions, precepts, strategies, and plans in our lives.

Faith is...

Bill Johnson says that faith moves heaven so that heaven will move earth. I like that. Bill goes on to say that faith is the atmosphere of experiencing truth.

Faith is also a revelation. John 16:13 tells us that the Holy Spirit will tell us things to come. In the Holiday Bowl story, it was going to rain in San Diego regardless; yet in the Lake Tahoe story, I felt we had an open door to pray the snow storm away. It took faith in both cases to make decisions. What if we had canceled the trip to San Diego and then five weeks later on game day we discovered that it was a bright sunny day? Faith is not a rationale based on natural things. Rather, faith is a canal based on spiritual things. The canal of God is filled with faith-filled believers flowing in and with the river of God to its next destination.

Faith is actually a destination that wraps the believers with robes of righteousness that we already discussed in the previous chapter. It takes a righteous person in Jesus to understand faith, to move in faith, and to operate in faith. That righteousness is not earned but given freely to everyone who will believe in Jesus as the Son of God and the Savior from their sins.

Most of you are probably like me in that you like to analyze some things that come into your life before you really pray about them. I am learning to pray first and trust God, forgetting the analyzing altogether. But I do believe that many believers overanalyze things to the point that they actually increase unbelief and doubt when they do get around to praying. I believe that many have analysis to the point of paralysis, and it is at that point that all of our anointed effective energy is completely zapped and we must get recharged or rebooted before we can proceed.

Here are some biblical examples of godly instructions that, if analyzed, everyone around that situation would probably have missed the presence, protection, or provision of God:

- Dip in a pool seven times.
- Walk around the walls, blowing the trumpets.
- Lay your hands on the sick.
- What do you have? Five thousand people will be fed with your small amount of fish and bread.
- Wait in Jerusalem for the Holy Spirit.
- Build an ark.

<u>For me, the instructions have sounded like this:</u>

- Give your car away when you only had one car.
- Give your rural country property away.
- Have your wife resign from teaching before she is pregnant, in faith that she will become pregnant.
- Give $1000 to a national ministry the first month your wife is not working.
- Tell a lady in Columbus, Ohio, to eat bananas for healing of chronic back pain.
- Command healing to flow—speak it, don't ask for it.
- Go to a stranger and tell that person not to sell the motor home but to use it in ministry instead.
- Ask a woman when she is going to finish the book of which she wrote three chapters twenty years prior.

- Double tithe for three months when there is no anticipated income.
- Tell the Vineyard pastor that he had been in a car accident forty years prior and that God is now healing his knee.
- Proclaim to the person with cancer in her leg that is scheduled to be amputated that God has healed her leg and the cancer is now shrinking.
- Speak to the eyes and command them to read.

Most of these stories have been written about in my previous books, so I won't share them now, but let me just add that with each new step of faith comes a great commitment to being responsible with what He shares with me. Each new level of trust is from God because the Lord does indeed order the steps of the righteous. Our steps are definitely being ordered with an direction that is taking us to new places with Him. It is a journey, for sure, and at times it is very difficult to trust in tough times, but also a journey that is well, well, well worth it. I know I overemphasized this, but it was for good reason. As we dig deep into the wells of faith and salvation, we discover that the water is fresher and cleaner too. It takes time and effort, but the overall value is worth it as well.

It Happens All the Time

Sometimes, I feel like Progressive Insurance when it comes to strange and unusual commands from the Lord: "It happens to me all the time." My wife will tell you that she believes I have a weather anointing. I just actually listen to God and pray storms and snow away and rain and sun into existence when given permission from Him. It's based entirely on what He is saying at the time. If He says, "Don't pray," I simply trust Him and don't pray. Sometimes it takes more faith to not pray then it does to pray. This happened recently in Omaha with a forecasted storm slated to hit on a Sunday, projecting many pastors to cancel their church services. God instructed me not to pray and just watch Him in action. Our service was delayed by twenty minutes, but we enjoyed an amazing time of entering His presence.

Abiding faith attracts the promises of God and releases His action plan in our lives and the lives of those we are praying for too. This, in turn, attracts the Holy Spirit to us in ways such as waves of glory, waves of healing, and waves of power. These effective prayers are faith-filled and energy-filled prayers that really do avail much, accomplish much, and attract the presence of the Lord in each situation and each category or situation that we are praying.

Your righteous effective prayers are filled with the energy of heaven that others need. Don't decline God's invitation and don't resist the opportunity to build His Kingdom right where you are today. I have frequently stated and written that trust is a must. Will you trust Him today? Will you heed the call? Will you respond with a resounding, "Yes," and shout, "Sign me up"?

I want to energize your world effectively with His anointed world. It's a decision that I know you won't regret. Just forget the past, reach forward, and press into all that God has for you this day, this month, and this year. I believe you will be amazed at where you are with Jesus at the conclusion of just one year if you will make that commitment and follow through. Remember, emotion often gets people to sign up but commitment gets them to show up.

Elijah was a man. And whether you are female or male, you are of the man species. So when I write that Elijah was a man, I can conclude that so are you.

Well, well, well, do you see any clouds?

Eighth Checkup
This Is a Great Day to Get Well

As I write this chapter, I want you to know that you have permission to get well at any time you are reading. You don't have to wait until you finish the book or even this chapter because this is a great day to get well. In fact, let me pray for you right now.

Father, I ask for Your presence to come and touch the person reading this book right now, and if they have any illness, any pain, any physical problem with them or a family member, I speak and write healing to them right now and declare that the illness must stop, cease, and vanish. I pray for healing and for a healing anointing to touch them now with Your presence and to bring restoration, good health, and total healing to them today in the name of Jesus. Amen.

Unusual Progression

This is one of the most unusual testimonies that God has opened up for me. I posted on the Facebook page of my friend Amos (who now lives in Arkansas), asking him if he knew I was planting a church in Omaha. Some lady on his page questioned me about this, and I then discovered that this lady lives close to us here in Nebraska. I told her a bit about the church plant and stated that I would be holding a meeting that evening at Panera Bread to share the blueprint with some interested folks, and she said that she too had a business meeting that night at the very same time at the very same Panera Bread!

After her meeting was finished, she came over and joined our meeting, with questions and discussion about the Kingdom of God. She brought a friend with her who was suffering with back pain. The lady who had back pain goes to a church that does not believe in healing for today. However, after some sharing of testimonies and a few Scriptures, I offered to pray for her and then asked her to walk across the restaurant. Most of the pain left. Then I asked the lady who saw my Facebook post to pray for her friend, and she got even better.

Kingdom Encounters

What are the odds of my posting on the page of a friend in Arkansas who had someone read it and comment, and we both have meetings at the same restaurant at the same time, and then we meet, and she learns how to pray for her friend who gets well? Sounds like a Kingdom encounter to me!

By the way, as this testimony was unfolding, it was the first day after our new church plant launched here in Omaha called Kingdom Encounters. Part of the DNA of this plant is to equip and teach others to do the same kinds of things Jesus did. Our goal is not so much about membership but rather about discipleship. This is demonstrated through our four agreement distinctions that we call Splash Zones because we believe that life in the river of God is fun.

I just taught in a recent service that God can and wants to move through technology and social media too. Case in point is a friend in Houston who, upon reading my Facebook note written above, asked for prayer for her wrenched foot that she could not walk on or even stand on. I then wrote out a prayer on Facebook, and she read it. I told her that there is a miracle when you check, so she stood up on her feet with no pain. She began to walk slowly, and in seconds stated she was fifty percent better. In an hour, she said she was eighty percent better. She also added that her mother had already scheduled an x-ray for her because of the severe pain she was experiencing, plus the inability to walk at all. The end result was she still went to the doctor and still had the x-ray, but God intervened and healed this condition much more quickly than she anticipated.

What happened was that God used our faith coupled with written prayers to see His manifested healing flow into her life. But

Eighth Checkup: This Is a Great Day to Get Well

it started with a set of unusual circumstances from the night before in Arkansas, to Nebraska, and then to Texas, and most likely way beyond that too as God keeps moving through one testimony to another. Revelation 19:10 says that the testimony of Jesus is the spirit of prophecy. When one person reads a testimony, it can instantly become a prophetic word that then releases a miracle into the reader or hearer of the testimony and enables God to move supernaturally in that person as well.

Political Realm

As stated in the foreword, Fc Farwell and I were invited to spend Election Day 2014 with a governor in another state. This governor and I have been friends for awhile, and as you know from reading a previous chapter, Fc is a trusted friend and a pastoral staff member of Kingdom Encounters. Fc prays for and sees many healings and enables others to pray and do the same.

After our time with the governor and some of his staff at the capitol, we went to a larger hotel in the host city where many of the members of all the political parties were having their gatherings with their constituents and awaiting the vote tally. Fc and I started mingling and meeting total strangers to discover how we could pray for them. I met a young couple who were working as temps for the company providing food that evening. They had recently moved to that area from Portland, Oregon, and they were new parents having a baby at home as well.

The young man's name was Joseph, and he was born with an ear problem that he already had multiple surgeries on and yet still was partially deaf in his right ear. I shared a couple other testimonies, quoting from Revelation 19:10 and explaining it to him. I then asked if I could pray for his ear. He agreed. Our location for prayer was in a very busy and noisy hallway, and my friend Fc was with me.

As I began to pray, I asked for the presence of the Lord and declared healing for about twenty seconds, and then told him there was a miracle when you check. I had him turn his back to me and cover his good ear with his hand, and I began to state random colors while I slowly backed away from him. After each color named, I asked him to repeat back to me what he heard. I was able to move about twelve to fourteen feet away from him, and he named every one of the colors correctly. Fc was standing next to Joseph and verified that he got them all correct. Again, I want to emphasize how noisy this area was, with people milling about and walking from one candidate's room to another while visiting with their friends.

Joseph sent me a couple emails a few days later to inform me that his ear was still well and wanted to thank me for the time we spent with him. He stated that he had never had anyone that he did not know give him that much attention and that much care and that he was truly grateful.

Then, just a few days later here in Omaha, I was meeting with a friend of mine named Mark. He had been having partial deafness in his right ear as well. There on the sidewalk, in front of Sozo Coffeehouse on a semi-busy street, I prayed a very short prayer for him, and he also covered his good ear and he too got all the colors correct as I backed away from him about ten feet. God is amazing, but we have to be willing to take that step of faith and to check things out. My friend Kris Kildosher from Bethel Church in Redding, California, taught me that there is a miracle when you check, and in each case and whenever possible, I ask people to check it out to see and experience the power of the answered prayer.

As I previously stated in another chapter, Bible study without Bible experience is pointless. When I am talking to someone about healing, I usually quote a Bible passage or two, so in essence, we have had Bible study. Then comes the experience through the manifested prayer time.

We are seeing consistent and regular joyful miracles in our new church plant, with folks stepping out in faith each week to pray for total strangers, and they too are seeing miracles, signs, and wonders as God shows up. As I write this, the congregation is growing in their understanding of what a Kingdom encounter is and how to navigate through it when visiting, sharing, witnessing, and praying with others. It is a joy to see and appreciate God's

Eighth Checkup: This Is a Great Day to Get Well

power moving in extraordinary ways through ordinary people. We do have a Kingdom Encounters page on Facebook, so feel free to drop in, read the testimonies, and get acquainted.

Supernatural

One of the cool testimonies that just recently happened was with a dear friend of mine, Sharon Fowler, who sits on my board of directors for Anointed 2 GO MdM and is a leader for us at Kingdom Encounters. Sharon was scheduled to have knee replacement surgery, but about two weeks before it was scheduled, I suggested to her that we pray, and she agreed. Again, it was literally about a thirty-second prayer, and I asked her to walk up and down some steps in the home where we were having our home group. She had no pain at all.

Later that week, she stated that she tried over and over to make her knee hurt but could not get it to do anything but be pain free. She was scheduled to see her doctor because he had scheduled pre-op blood work for her, but when she went in she asked to speak to the doctor first. She then sat in a chair and bent her legs way back under the chair and then got up and jumped up and down several times. She then told him that I had prayed for her and that she thought she was well. He checked her out more and agreed that she was well and promptly canceled the surgery. Even beyond that, God also healed her vertigo and shortness of breath, which she had also been experiencing for several months, and we did not even pray for those items. Isn't God good? Someone shout Hallelujah! I think that was a whisper—try again. Go ahead, I know you want to—let 'er rip!

I was just at a local coffee shop in Omaha and saw a woman limping, so when I had an opportunity, I struck up a conversation with her and asked why she was limping. She stated that she has bad arthritis in her knee, so I then shared Sharon's testimony with her and asked if I could pray. She agreed. After forty-five seconds of prayer, I asked her to walk across the room, and her face beamed with a big smile as she let me know that almost all the pain had suddenly disappeared. She was elated. I prayed one more time and walked with her while proclaiming healing, and she got even better.

Over and over, we consistently see these things happening as we step out in faith and simply invite God to show up with His very presence. Sometimes our only available transportation is a leap of faith. Like Elijah, I am only a man. You need to understand that I am no one special. You need to understand that I am no one special. Bet you thought that is an error, but I stated it twice to emphasize that I am not anyone special, but I am a believer in Someone Who is, and His name is Jesus. (Plus, I have a signature of stating something twice in every book, and this seemed like a good place to do this. I learned this from a brick layer friend years ago named David Palm who always turned one brick different in a job as his signature on that brick laying job).

Jesus has a signature too, and it is called *finished*. He does not leave anything undone. It may not be finished the way we think it should be, or in the time frame that fits our schedule or desire, but His ways are higher, different, and not always consistent with what we think is normal. The signature of Jesus is His stamp of approval. When Jesus says He will do something, you can count on it being completed. I love Philippians 1:6 because I see a lot of two- and three-day miracles, and this verse is what I often quote to others who only experience a partial healing after prayer: "Being confident of this very thing, that He who has begun a good work in you will complete it until the day of Jesus Christ." By the way, it is my belief that Jesus never rested because He was tired, but only when He was finished.

Authentication

God's Word authenticates His actions. He promises in the Bible that his Word will not return void, but it will accomplish that which He sent it to accomplish. He set this pattern up from the very beginning in Genesis 1:1–3: "In the beginning God created the heavens and the earth. The earth was without form, and void; and darkness was on the face of the deep. And the Spirit of God

Eighth Checkup: This Is a Great Day to Get Well

was hovering over the face of the waters. Then God said, 'Let there be light'; and there was light."

The word *hovering* means "to think deeply." While hovering over the face of the deep, God was thinking deeply, but nothing happened until He spoke. When He spoke, that which He spoke came into being. Then He named what He had just spoken. I practice this same sequence when praying for the sick, in that I don't just pray for the sick, but I speak it and name it by calling the person well. Sometimes, I emphasize it by raising my voice a bit and declaring in a positive life-giving, health-producing way: "Well! Well! Well!" Those are not questions, but statements of belief. You are *well*!

In this passage from Genesis, God sets up a prophetic pattern that will continue into Revelation with the process of speaking, calling things into existence, and then naming that which was spoken. He thought it! He spoke it! He saw it! And He named it! This is a great day to get well. Do you agree?

The Kingdom of God is voice-activated and touch-imparted. We speak that which God is calling us to speak, and we touch that which God is calling us to touch. Either way, He gets the glory, and the people get assistance. And I'm happy with that.

Let me add to this by sharing that a thought is a word unspoken, but a word is a manifested thought. The word *manifest* means to be made known, to reveal, to bring into the light, and to become conspicuous. God loves to manifest His presence, which then brings everything into the light: His Light. He is the Light! Light shines when God shows up, and darkness flees away. James 1:17 declares, "Every good and perfect gift is from above, and comes down from the Father of Lights, with whom there is no variation or shadow of turning." In other words, if you could look at God like you look at anything else that is above you, say, a grandstand light at an outdoor concert or the tall poles that hold the lights for a nighttime tennis match, you would not see a dark shadow anywhere. With natural lights on a pole, you would be able to find shadows, but when you look at God, the only shadow you see is that of light because the shadow of God is light, not dark. Jesus is the Light of the world. If you want to get rid of darkness anywhere around you, just ask Jesus to show up, and the darkness will begin to be dispelled and eventually totally disappear as the Light takes over.

No Luck Needed

So, too, in praying for others, we can pray that the Light of Jesus will invade the darkness of sickness and push it out so that the healing power of Jesus can then invade the same area and bring healing. As I already stated, how He chooses to do that is His business. He may do it supernaturally or gradually over time or even through the hands of doctors. It's His deal, and we are not playing cards either. There is no luck involved here as there is with the luck of the draw. Jesus does not operate from a posture of luck because, in that realm, someone always loses; but in God's realm, no one loses. So don't bother praying for any gambling wager you may have made as those prayers will go unanswered because they are based on iniquity. Psalm 66:18 declares that if we regard iniquity in our heart, the Lord won't hear us.

The word *luck* is really a derivative from the word *lucifer*, and yes I intentionally did not capitalize his name. We choose to operate from a position of blessing and don't need or want any luck at all. So don't go thinking that all you have is bad luck because of your situation. If you are a believer in Jesus you are on the side of Light; whereas luck is on the side of darkness. We choose to stand on the side of blessing and operate in the realm of blessings.

Psalm 103 lists many of these blessings as benefits. In verse three we are told that two of these blessings are that He forgives all our iniquities and heals all our diseases. This is Old Testament under the Law, so how much more applicable is the love, anointing, and healing power of Jesus under the New Testament, which includes avenues of grace and more grace? I am learning that sometimes all I need to pray is for more grace and then healing also manifests. Grace has so many benefits too. We are covered over with such great blessings through Jesus and the ministry of grace. So we endeavor to walk with Him each day, and

Eighth Checkup: This Is a Great Day to Get Well

if we encounter sickness or illness, we can honestly say that this is a great day to get well.

Ninth Checkup
Intercession, Revelation, Manifestation

Well, well, well, you are probably thinking that I finally got around to a chapter specifically about prayer, but the reality is that I have been talking about prayer all through this book. But you are right: This chapter deals with some specifics of prayer. I realize that there are probably more books written about prayer than any other Christian discipline, yet it seems to be one of the hardest things for believers to grasp onto and participate in on a consistent basis. Often, after just a few minutes, we may feel like we are completely worn out and that we have exhausted God in the process. While our intentions are good, we need to learn how to persevere and break through in prayer. It is not an easy task, but it is a worthwhile task, for sure.

Another aspect of prayer is that of waiting. I wrote a chapter about this in my first book *Downloads from Heaven*, but some of that bears repeating as we grow and learn what God is doing in our lives and in the lives of others for whom we are interceding. First, let's just examine the word *intercession*. "Inter-" means "to go into and dwell within," and "-cession" means "to surrender." When we participate in intercession, we go into and dwell with God with the idea of surrendering our will, our ways, and our strategies to His. Our goal in prayer is not to convince God to see it our way, but to respond to what He is doing. We often say at Kingdom Encounters that we embrace what God is doing, not what He is not doing.

Praying Past the Past

Let me share an example. In chapter six I mentioned that at times, when dealing with Paul's letter to the Philippians where he said to forget the past, reach forward, and press ahead, we may have to deal specifically with yokes of hereditary influence and family strongholds in order to get past those things that hold us back from entering into the present things God has for us. I remember once when ministering in Puerto Rico that a lady came forward for prayer after the preaching and ministry of the Word of God. Her arm was in a sling, and she had ongoing numbness and pain. I prayed for her a couple times, but nothing seemed to be happening.

I then asked if her mother had this condition and learned that she had; and then I asked if her grandmother also had this same condition, and she too previously dealt with the same issue. So I prayed against a generational curse and broke the power of that curse that was somehow moving from generation to generation. In a very short amount of time that evening, her arm was out of the sling and she had full mobility and movement of her arm without any pain. In fact, it was so noticeable to others in that traditional Lutheran church that some of the leaders approached me and apologized for trying to get me to teach and preach on a more traditional subject rather than the anointing that the pastor had asked me to teach on. They were amazed to see that this lady who had been in obvious pain for many years was now set free simply through a prayer of deliverance from a generational curse.

Not only did the prayer bring healing to this lady, but it also brought an openness to the leaders of the congregation to want more of the Holy Spirit's activity in their church. Another time at a local church in the Omaha area, I was leading a healing service and felt led to pray for people with pain in their shoulders and necks, and everyone in the room got well except for a fifteen-year-old girl. We prayed and anointed her with oil and rebuked the illness and laid our hands on her shoulder, but nothing seemed to work. So I stopped the service and asked God for wisdom. James 1:5 tells us that if we ask God for wisdom, He will give it to us. In just a

Ninth Checkup: Intercession, Revelation, Manifestation

few moments, I knew what the problem was and went up to her and prayed against a generational curse. Immediately, her pain left her and she could move freely. I did not actually pray for her healing but instead dealt with the main problem, and the symptoms vanished.

As the title of this chapter promotes, I believe that intercession brings revelation and that revelation brings manifestation. In both of these previous examples, that is exactly what happened. Through prayer and asking for wisdom, God revealed the problem, and then the healing just showed up. There was a blockage that needed to be dealt with, and when that wall was removed, the obvious easy answer just moved right in, and the healing result that so many had prayed for showed up with ease.

Hindrances and Blockades

There are hindrances to some prayers being answered. For instance, as I mentioned in a previous chapter, Psalm 66:18 says that if we regard iniquity in our heart, the Lord won't hear us. It doesn't say that if we regard sin in our hearts, the Lord won't hear us. Iniquity is different from sin. Sin is simply missing the mark. It is an archery term used to describe how, even with good intentions and proper aim, the target is not hit due to other circumstances. The Bible makes it clear that all have sinned and fall short of the glory of God (Rom. 3:23). Jesus became sin so that we could become righteous. But even in that state of righteousness, if we give regard to iniquity, we run the risk that God won't hear our prayer. So then, what is iniquity?

Iniquity is ongoing, intentional sin. When people repent of the sin of iniquity, there is a tendency for some to be thinking that they'll do it again anyway. It can be compared to the cud that a cow chews over and over and somehow drops that cud into one of seven stomachs and then brings it back up to chew on repeatedly. Iniquity, if not sincerely dealt with, can and often will prevent God from moving effectively in certain areas of life. Grace goes a long ways, and we know that His mercies are definitely new every morning. However, repentance for the blotting out of our sins, along with enjoying times of refreshing from the presence of the Lord as outlined in Acts 3:19, is certainly important. Acts 3:19 also challenges us to be converted in our prayers of repentance. When we are fully engaged with that conversion process, iniquity will disappear from our lives.

In 1 Peter 3:7 men are told to honor their wives so that their prayers are not hindered. I often share with men and challenge them to honor their wives. Some men like to poke fun at their wives or tell jokes about them or slam them for their looks, weight, hairstyle, and so on. All of these traits do not bring honor, but instead dishonor them. And then the men often wonder why their connection to God in prayer seems to be lacking what it previously had in power and authority. Beating up your wife verbally is an indication that your prayers are indeed going to be hindered from receiving the answer that you need. These hindrances here and in Psalm 66 are not all-inclusive of what could block your prayers from being answered, but they are a good place to start.

Whether you are a man or a woman, if you are lacking revelation or wisdom on how to proceed after praying for something for a long time, it might be a good time to have some personal introspection on the conversion process of repentance. As we repent of our sins, God is gracious and will forgive us our sins and cleanse us from all unrighteousness, including iniquity. This will then set us up to experience more consistent answers to prayer.

The word *introspection* from the dictionary means to have a reflective inward look with an examination of one's own thoughts and feelings. The etymology of this word is continued by adding the word *scope*, which is an instrument used for viewing things closely. As with perspective, introspection has the word *spec* hidden in the middle, and a spec was the old school abbreviated term for a spectacle worn in the eye to help bring focus for vision, just as glasses do today.

Perspective brings two common phrases together to help bring understanding and clarify. These are: "look out" and "outlook." Look out simply means to watch for something; whereas, outlook is a state of mind that brings in anticipation with anxiousness and concern or great joy and encouragement. So as we

Ninth Checkup: Intercession, Revelation, Manifestation

pray and experience introspection, we might discover things that perhaps are not pleasing to the Lord, perhaps even blockages; yet with God's grace, love, and forgiveness flowing, we then can easily move to a perspective that ushers in joy and encouragement as we proceed with God's strategy, plan, and enthusiasm for how He plans to work this situation out in our lives.

Listed below are a few testimonies of answered prayer from an acquaintance of mine in Omaha, written in his own words:

The Gift Card

My Mom and I occasionally talk about how God helps us in situations where we've either misplaced or lost an item or how He nudges us to go check on something. Last Christmas I gave my wife a $100 Target gift card. A few weeks later she wanted it to go shopping. We searched everywhere, every room of the house, kid's toy box, saved Christmas tissue paper, bows, and boxes...everywhere. After looking off and on for over a week, we both had this bad feeling it had been thrown out with the trash on Christmas morning.

One afternoon I had gone back in to the storage room of our basement and looked through all of the Christmas boxes one more time. No gift card. That's when I realized, even though it felt like a stupid thing to do (to waste the Almighty's time with this), I prayed. I told Jesus that He knows where that gift card is and asked for Him to either place it where I will find it or to reveal its location to me.

I waited in silence for a couple of minutes, and nothing came to me. So, I walked up the stairs and met my wife in the kitchen. She asked if I had been searching through the Christmas stuff for that gift card. I told her I had, I didn't find it, and so I finally broke down and prayed about it. I told her what I had prayed and as the words "reveal its location to me" came out of my mouth, it was done! God had instantly downloaded that information to me just like that!

I sprinted up the stairs and ran into my office, picked up a business envelope that was lying on the back of the desk, opened it up, and there was that $100 gift card. I was stunned and humiliated at the same time. I felt so bone-headed because I forgot that I put it right where it needed to be, and also stunned that God actually took the time to help me with such a trivial request.

Having God download to me is something that never gets old. It is refreshing in a sense that God's downloads remind me of my relationship with Him, that we are in constant communication and that it's a connection that once you experience it, you want more of it!

The Snowblower

As the first major winter storm was approaching, I wanted to move my larger two-stage snowblower from the shed in the backyard up to the garage so that it was ready to go the next morning. After putting gas in the tank and priming the engine, I pulled, and pulled, and pulled again on that rope, trying to get it started. I hadn't used the snowblower since the previous spring when I "summerized" it for storage. It's a newer snowblower with less than a hundred hours on it, and it had always started with only one or two pulls of the rope.

Ninth Checkup: Intercession, Revelation, Manifestation

After many unsuccessful attempts inside the shed, I dragged the snowblower up the hill and into the garage. I pulled the spark plug and examined it. There was fuel getting to it. I check the air filter, and it was clean, so I tripled-checked the choke and ignition—all were in the correct position for ignition. Then, I pulled and pulled and pulled again, but not even a sputter! Ugh.

After about thirty minutes of this mounting frustration, I finally sat down to rest. That's when it dawned on me: I hadn't used Jesus. Now, even for a mature believer like myself, I thought invoking the power in the name of Jesus to start my snowblower was crazy. But, I relented and decided why not, so I got back up.

I laid my hands on the engine and declared, "By the power in the blood and name of Jesus Christ, start!" I pulled the rope and it almost started. Whoa! A sputter. I declared again even louder, "By the power in the blood and name of Jesus Christ, start!" I pulled the rope and the snowblower roared to life! Wow!

As crazy as that sounds, that was a faith-building moment for me. I knew that no matter what it is in life, Jesus is there and ready to help out.

The Parking Spot

Where I work, we employ over two thousand people, and there are no parking garages. The building is surrounded by multiple parking lots. At the farthest distance, you might end up walking about a quarter of a mile. When the weather is nice, I don't mind parking far away because I enjoy the walk. However, during bitterly cold Nebraska winters, even the shortest walk can be brutal. With wind chills so cold, skin begins to freeze in just five to ten minutes.

So during one extremely cold week, I started asking God for a parking space to be open for me as close as possible to the doors. When I would arrive, sure enough, there was one open space near the front. I didn't need to pray this every morning because if I left the house early enough, spots were normally available. However, on those bitterly cold mornings I was running late, a simple prayer had God saving me a close parking space.

The Foot Pain

One day at work I had somehow stepped wrong on my left foot and pulled either a muscle or tendon in my arch and the ball of my foot. It was painful to walk on, but I figured the pain would go away. By that evening, the pain had turned into a terrible ache. I knew I had pulled or partially torn a tendon or something. Whatever it was, my foot still hurt and ached worse than before. The pain kept me awake for a few hours until finally around 1:30 in the morning, I took two aspirin, and as I crawled back into bed, I simply asked God to take the pain away.

He then told me to get back out of bed and walk to the end of our hallway and back. I thought, *"This is crazy, it's late, and I'm imagining this."* I was then reminded what I had learned from a friend (Jay West) who has the anointing power of healing. He said there are results if you check. So, I finally

Ninth Checkup: Intercession, Revelation, Manifestation

decided to get out of bed to do what I thought God was telling me to do.

As I began walking down the hallway, the joints in my left foot popped loudly, and there was a sharp pain that shot through my whole foot, and then the pain went away as I reached the end of the hallway. As I walked back to my bedroom, there was just a hint of a dull ache, but major relief! I then quickly fell asleep. When I woke up later that morning, my foot had some slight soreness, but overall felt pretty good. Knowing I had a busy day planned, I took an eight hundred milligram Motrin and assumed I'd be taking another one with lunch. I never did.

It wasn't until later that evening that I realized I had been pain-free all day long. I then thought to myself that God is probably shaking His head and rolling His eyes at me. Here I am in pain that's keeping me awake, I ask God for help, then when He tells me to check, and I nearly ignore Him. God's ways are not our ways, and faith is in things not seen. Lesson learned!

Pray First

These are all great testimonies and messages about prayer, introspection, and how intercession brings revelation which in turn brings manifestation. In chapter eight, you learned that the word *manifest* means to be made known, brought to the light, revealed, and made conspicuous. We see in each of these examples, and many previous ones in this book, how that process is revealed. And each time it happens, it changes our outlook. It may even cause us to stop and ponder with the words, "Well, well, well, look what just happened." I wonder what would have happened if I had prayed first. Have you ever thought that?

As we learn and grow, we discover our approach changes, and we begin to include God in things from the very beginning, rather than waiting until near the end when it might be too late. I am always startled when I hear of people who, on the day before a surgery or the day before a major medical event, suddenly run into church and ask us to pray so that they don't have to go through the procedure. I get it, in that most don't want the expense, the recovery time, and the costs and inconvenience that it causes. Yet often we will discover that this situation has been going on for weeks and sometimes months, but this is the first we are hearing of the prayer need. What is it that keeps people from praying as the first option rather than waiting until it is the last option?

When I used to travel and speak about prayer at churches, I often encouraged boards and committees to start with prayer, asking for God's vision from the very beginning. On the contrary, though, my normal experience is that most church boards, building committees, and planning groups go through hours and hours of planning and strategy, and finally, when they are ready to launch, they ask for God's blessing. But what if that is not God's plan for them at all? What if, by doing what they saw the Father doing, as recorded in John 5:19, they simply came together and asked the Lord what His plan was and then began to work out that plan? Like I said in an earlier chapter, Martha was busy making sandwiches and soup that perhaps Jesus never asked for.

Four Houses

Let's look together at a passage from Matthew 21:12–16:

> Then Jesus went into the temple of God and drove out all those who bought and sold in the temple, and overturned the tables of the money changers and the seats of those who sold doves. And He said to them, "It is written, 'My house shall be called a house of prayer,' but you have made it a 'den of thieves.'"

Ninth Checkup: Intercession, Revelation, Manifestation

> Then the blind and the lame came to Him in the temple, and He healed them. But when the chief priests and scribes saw the wonderful things that He did, and the children crying out in the temple and saying, "Hosanna to the Son of David!" they were indignant and said to Him, "Do You hear what these are saying?" And Jesus said to them, "Yes. Have you never read, 'Out of the mouth of babes and nursing infants You have perfected praise'?"

This story introduces some introspection from Jesus as He enters the temple and discovers it is not being utilized in its original intent and for the purposes of honoring God. Jesus cleanses the temple, and it is an external picture of an internal process that He also offers to us. The difference is, of course, that the violence He used in overturning the tables and chasing everyone out was completed for us on the Cross when Jesus endured all of the punishment and violence for our sake so that we don't have to go through that. All we need to do is turn and repent (Acts 3:19).

There are four houses represented in this text. In verse twelve we discover a house of purity, which is followed by a house of prayer in verse thirteen. This takes us to a house of power in verse fourteen and ultimately leads to a house of praise in verses fifteen and sixteen. Is your body, which is the temple of the Holy Spirit, a house of purity, coupled with a house of prayer that leads you to a house of power that concludes with a house of praise, or are you simply a den of thieves? In this case, a den of thieves is a place where the enemy makes camp and steals the presence of God from you so that you want anything but God and usually only go to Him as a last resort. If and when you pray, you rarely see any power and wonder why things always seem to go badly for you. Maybe as you read this you know of someone who experiences these things. Will you be bold enough to approach them and to challenge them to clean house? Will you take the lessons learned so far and proceed with a new outlook that says things can be different? Or will you be content to respond and say, "Well, well,

well, it may work for Pastor Jay and all of these others that I have read about so far, but it doesn't work for me"? The choice is entirely yours. The ball is in your court. Time is about to expire. What will be your best shot at changing things in your life? How will you proceed?

I hope it is on the side of prayer and intercession. I hope it is on the Kingdom playing field and not in the stands, watching someone else getting to play and enjoy the benefits of God. I hope it is one in which you want to participate to the fullest with the anointing of God flowing in your life to truly make a difference in the lives of others, while advancing the Kingdom of God.

The title of this chapter is "Intercession, Revelation, Manifestation." But there is one more word that I want to share, and that is *exaltation*. Remember my friend's examples and how joyful he was that certain things worked out when he prayed. The manifestation brings exaltation. We get excited when we see God working things out, and we want to give Him praise. The same theme was happening in the Matthew 21 passage, where the last house was one of praise. Once the manifestation happens, once the power is displayed and things begin to turn around, our naturally supernatural response is one of praising and exalting God, giving exaltation to the One Who brought the solution, the healing, and/or whatever answer was needed at the time.

Intercession brings revelation. Revelation brings manifestation. Manifestation brings exaltation. And exaltation returns us to intercession. That is the pattern. Jesus went from one prayer meeting to another and did ministry in between. He then went back to prayer to discover from the Father what the next step was. If you want to move in the power of God and see the miraculous happen on a consistent basis, you must be a person who prays.

Tenth Checkup
More on Intercession

As I was completing the writing of the previous chapter, it occurred to me that my son Jason had a good chapter in his first book that would tie in well with what I had just written, so with his permission, I am sharing chapter six called "The Prayer of Power" from his book *Who Will Ascend? Taking Prayer to Another Level.*

But before I do that, I want to emphasize the importance of staying fresh with God. By fresh, I mean in a relationship where He is speaking to you, you are hearing His voice, you are accustomed to what His voice sounds like, and you have a good relationship with Him that is growing in faith daily with new challenges that present new opportunities for courage. Yet, you also realize that you know that God is with you and has your back. Every day I pray for a fresh anointing on my life, according to Psalm 92:10. I can't rely on yesterday's anointing or a previous method, so, like Jesus, I need to know what my Father is doing and respond to His beckoning and His initiatives. Most of us have experienced a time when we purchased some fruit and cut it open, thinking it was fresh, only to discover that it was either not quite ripe yet or way too ripe. In both cases, it was uneatable in its present form. We need to be presentable as Kingdom representatives, ready to pray and to offer ministry in season and out, and to be responsive to the call of our Father's words when He issues them to us.

Just this week, I had a business meeting with someone whom I had never met regarding some insurance coverage. When we were wrapping up our time, I asked if I could pray with this person, and she was very grateful, asking prayer for personal needs in her family. Later that morning, I was at my lawyer's office, and I had an opportunity to bring up prayer with the receptionist, and she too asked me to pray for personal family issues. Later in the evening, I was at a local restaurant, and as my friends and I were getting ready to leave, I asked our waitress if she needed prayer, and she asked for discernment for her husband and herself, as they were looking for a new church home. I shared my church business card with her and prayed that God would lead them to the right place. In between those times of prayer, I was at other locations in the greater Omaha area, but God did not prompt me to pray for anyone at those locations.

Staying Fresh

Being fresh simply means to be ready at the right season. And yes, I know I quoted above about being ready out of season so let me explain that. Even if I don't feel like praying, I am on call with the Lord 24/7. I may sense it is a season of rest, but if the season is right or ripe for the person He is asking me to pray into, then I need to be ready. Here is how hope is released: God is omnipresent, so He is in the future where a promise of His will be fulfilled in my life or someone else's. He goes to that point and brings back the promise of completion from that point to where we are now and gives us that promise as a prophetic word of completion. When that happens, hope arises and springs up in our lives.

Proverbs 13:12 says that hope deferred makes the heart sick, but when it springs forth it is a tree of life. Romans 15:13 adds this: "Now may the God of hope fill you with all joy and peace in believing, that you may abound in hope by the power of the Holy Spirit." Much of our hope in prayer relies heavily on our relationship with Jesus. We are assured that He is with us, but we also want to know that His power is going to be there when we need it. This brings us to Jason's chapter, which I will share with you now:

The Prayer of Power[6]

Do you remember the three qualifications that make our prayers accomplish much? They are: effective,

Tenth Checkup: More on Intercession

fervent, and righteous. Now, let's examine them more thoroughly, in reverse order, starting with righteousness.

We can pray a lot about the desires of our hearts—even what we want our lives to become—but do we ever ask ourselves, "Where is my heart?" A great desire of my heart is to see revival come in this day and age. The Bible says, "Delight yourself in the Lord and He shall give you the desires of your heart" (Ps. 37:4). If my heart is not delighting in Him, then my heart's desire will not be fulfilled through Him. So, when we pray, where are our hearts? Do we stand pure, holy, and righteous before God?

This whole book is entitled *Who Will Ascend?* Remember the qualifications for ascending? They're found in Psalm 24:4: "He who has clean hands and a pure heart, who has not lifted up his soul to an idol, nor sworn deceitfully." Ascending the mountain of God (praying effectively) requires righteousness! All four of those qualifications require righteousness on our part. Remember, anyone can pray, but not anyone can ascend. Effective prayers come from righteous people.

The Psalm says, "If I regard iniquity in my heart, the Lord will not hear" (Ps. 66:18). The first step to widespread revival is personal revival. If our hearts are not right with God, the Bible says the Lord will not even hear our prayers, much less answer them. How can we pray for change in a nation when we won't allow the Lord to change us, individually? Truly, if we would allow Him to change each of us, the nation would be changed.

This is repentance: a sorrow for sin that produces change. It is the first step on the road to revival. James 5:16a tells us, "Confess your trespasses to one another, and pray for one another, that you may be healed." The healing that comes from confession of sins is not merely physical, but literally all-encompassing. When we confess our sins to one another and pray for one another, we will see such unity among us that our relationships will be healed. Our spiritual climate will be healed. Ultimately, our land will be healed.

This is righteousness: not the living without sin, but the repentance and confession of sin, combined with a change of heart that makes us desire to sin no more. Before going any further, this hurdle of righteousness must be addressed. Our prayers cannot be effective or fervent if we are not righteous. Our hearts must be right with God before He can give us our hearts' desires.

Take a moment right now to get right with God in your heart, repent of your sins, and seek His righteousness. This must be dealt with before we can move on. Then, continue reading as we discuss the other two qualifications of power-filled prayers.

* * *

Okay. Now, let's examine fervency and effectiveness in our prayers.

In addition to being birthed out of a righteous heart, Scripture says our prayers must be fervent in order to accomplish much. What does that look like? What does it mean? Well, I believe the most fervent prayers are faith-filled prayers. When we pray for

Tenth Checkup: More on Intercession

revival, we must have faith to believe it can actually happen.

I know many people who want to see revival come. In fact, one night while I was praying to God, I myself said, "God, I really want revival." Does anyone want to guess what I believe He said to me? I sensed He was telling me, "That's not enough." I wondered what He meant at first, but He went on: "This is not a question of your wanting revival; it's a question of what you are willing to do to attain it." That struck me. Anyone can want something; it doesn't take faith to want something. It *does* take faith to pursue it! I can want to win first place in the 400-meter dash in track, but if I don't run the race, I'll never get what I want. We've got to move out of our want-to mode and into our will-do mode. We must not just hope, wish, or dream about revival, as if it were something unattainable. If we really want it, we must run after God!

So often, we pray for revival to come but don't really expect it. We don't have active faith to back up our prayers. The prayer without faith is basically wishful thinking. God *can* and *does* make wishes come true, but He is activated by faith (see Mk. 5:3). James 5:15 says, "And the prayer of faith will save the sick." I challenge everyone: When we pray for revival, let's not say, "If it comes"; let's boldly declare, "When it comes"!

Now, one more component must be addressed in our effort to make our prayers accomplish much. James says that, in addition to being fervent prayers of righteous men, our prayers must be effective. So, what makes our prayers effective? I believe one key thing allows them to be effective: They must be in God's will.

We can be the most righteous people on earth, praying with all great faith, but if we are not praying God's will, we will not accomplish much. Our prayers are futile if what we're praying for is not in God's good and perfect will. Even Jesus, the most righteous Man of faith on earth, needed to keep in tune with the will of God. In Matthew 6:10, He teaches us to pray, "Your kingdom come. Your will be done on earth as it is in heaven." In the garden of Gethsemane, He prayed, "Saying, 'Father, if it is Your will, take this cup away from Me; nevertheless not My will, but Yours be done'" (Luke 22:42). We must strive to remain in God's will when we pray!

When our prayers are effective, fervent, and righteous, they are lethal weapons against the evil forces of the enemy! However, with one component missing, the prayers begin to lose that effectiveness. If we pray in faith but against the will of God, we'll either get no result or a crisis. What if we prayed with all faith for a mountain to move into the sea? If God were to allow this to happen outside His will (presuming that He *could* allow something to happen outside His will, which is a whole other debate!), there would be great disaster both for those living in the mountains and those living by the sea! We can think of the Israelites when they desperately asked God to give them a king. God answered their prayer; however, this answered prayer only led to disaster because God gave them what they wanted, not what He wanted.

Tenth Checkup: More on Intercession

On the other hand, if we pray with no faith but according to God's will, we'll either get no result or be very surprised. When Jesus told the disciples to cast their nets to the other side of the boat to catch more fish, they didn't have faith it would happen. Yet, it did—so much that their nets broke. Because they weren't prepared for what God said He would do, they were overwhelmed.

Remember Elijah? He prayed for rain out of a righteous heart, full of faith that it would happen, and according to the will of God. So, let's do likewise! Let's pray righteous prayers (out of a pure heart), fervent prayers (out of faith), and effective prayers (in God's will). If we do this, I believe we will never be the same! We will see change. We will see a miracle. We will see a revival of God's Presence with us!

Practically Speaking . . .

What is one way to increase the level of faith in your prayers? A key ingredient that causes faith to grow is the power of the testimony. By sharing testimonies of how God has worked in your life and by asking others to share their testimonies with you, I can guarantee that you will be encouraged and your faith will increase. Whenever I am lacking the faith I need to pray for something, I know that I only need to recall the testimonies of how God has divinely worked in the past in order to inspire me to pray concerning the future! Never underestimate the power in a testimony.

What is one way to increase your accuracy in praying according to God's will? Examine the motives behind the prayers you pray. Are you praying for what you want or what God wants? Hopefully, what you want is the same thing as what God wants. But I know that for me, that is not always the case. How do you discern the difference? A key way to discern the difference is to check everything with Scripture to see if it lines up with God's Word. In addition, seek confirmation from spiritual leaders in your life, and pray for peace to rest in your heart as a sign that you're on the right track.

Experiencing God

I hope you enjoyed reading some of Jason's first book. Jason loves to pray and serves with Diane and me as the Nebraska representatives for the United States Prayer Council. He was birthed in prayer, and that Kingdom quality remains in his life to this day.

Often, when I pray for people, one of the first sentences out of their mouths is, "Wow, I am experiencing such peace now." The enemy comes with distractions, turmoil, stress, anxiety, unrest, condemnation, and a host of other negative things that pull you and me away from God's peace. But when peace is there, we are assured that God is there.

In Mark 4:35–41 we see a great example of peace being displayed:

> On the same day, when evening had come, He said to them, "Let us cross over to the other side." Now when they had left the multitude, they took Him along in the boat as He was. And other little boats were also with Him. And a great windstorm arose, and the waves beat into the boat, so that it was already filling. But He was in the stern, asleep on a pillow. And they awoke Him and said to Him, "Teacher, do You not care that we are perishing?"

Tenth Checkup: More on Intercession

> Then He arose and rebuked the wind, and said to the sea, "Peace, be still!" And the wind ceased and there was a great calm. But He said to them, "Why are you so fearful? How *is it* that you have no faith?" And they feared exceedingly, and said to one another, "Who can this be, that even the wind and the sea obey Him!"

It was said of Jesus that He used peace to calm the storm and He also used peace to sleep through the storm. I've heard Bill Johnson say, "You only have peace in storms you can sleep through."

Never Settle

Up in the section of this chapter from Jason's book he wrote about Luke 22:42: "Nevertheless not My will, but Yours be done."

Nevertheless also appears in 2 Corinthians 7:5–7:

> For indeed, when we came to Macedonia, our bodies had no rest, but we were troubled on every side. Outside were conflicts, inside were fears. Nevertheless God, who comforts the downcast, comforted us by the coming of Titus, and not only by his coming, but also by the consolation with which he was comforted in you, when he told us of your earnest desire, your mourning, your zeal for me, so that I rejoiced even more.

Here is the picture: Paul is ministering and sharing how tired he was. Not only was he dead-dog tired, but there were conflicts, problems, fears, and a host of other negative things going on, but with courage Paul responds, "Nevertheless God." Say that out loud: "Nevertheless God." Say it again. Say it again. Now, shout it! Give God some glory because your breakthrough is near. When you understand that regardless of what the storm looks like, and it looks bad on every side, you are still able to respond, "Nevertheless God," then help is close.

Nevertheless God simply means, "Never settle for anything less than God." If that means pressing through for supernatural healing, then go for it. If that means rushing to the ER in the middle of the night, then do that. God will show Himself strong on your behalf. That promise is given to us in 2 Chronicles 16:9. He is more invested in your problem than you are. He is more interested in your healing than you are. And He is certainly more interested in you following His example of being able to sleep peacefully through your trials and storms so that you can be a living testimony to others who are about to do the same. I believe that Jesus is working behind the scenes on your behalf right now. Let's pray. You lead!

Eleventh Checkup
Unusual and Uncommon Un-Methods

Recently while ministering at Calvary Lutheran Church in Omaha, where my friend TW Norman is the pastor, we saw and experienced many healings and amazing things that God was doing in the house. I basically preached a new message regarding how, when you hear a testimony, it can release a prophetic work in you to receive a similar move of God in your life and produce another testimony in like fashion, while giving several examples plus Scripture verses to back it up. (Actually, I have already shared about this topic but am emphasizing it for the point of the stories.)

After sharing this message that included many testimonies, I asked those who were in pain to stand up, regardless of where the pain was, and I began to pray, inviting the presence of God into the room and into their situations. It basically started slowly but suddenly took off, with many people stating they were fifty or seventy-five percent better and demonstrating things that they couldn't do prior to the prayer, such as deep knee bends, moving arms and shoulders above their heads, moving their fingers, or walking smoothly and evenly. Some walked without their canes, and one lady, who I later found out is very shy, came to the front, smiling and walking up and down the altar steps with no pain and without her cane. It was awesome!

Another person stated that her jaw stopped hurting and clicking due to TMJ, and then another person stated that her knee stopped clicking. I later prayed for a man in the foyer, and he had substantial release of pain and more ease of movement in his knees. Many of the people stated it all started to happen as they heard some of the other testimonies in the service. In reality, much of the healing happened prior to any prayers being offered.

In the evening, the healings continued, and the man for whom I prayed in the foyer came up just to get in the presence of God. Not knowing that he had two hearing aids in, I asked him how his hearing was, and he told me and showed me the hearing aids. I began to pray for him and had my son Jason, who was leading worship, turn the mic off, and this man could still hear and understand the words. Then I had a friend of his stand near him and gradually walk away from him, saying colors in random order, and the man got every color correct. He told me after the service that his ears had improved and that he was leaving the hearing aids out.

Spontaneous Healing

I love spontaneous healing that happens when people are perhaps looking for one specific healing and then another one happens. Maybe they were not expecting healing at all, but just hanging around Jesus and getting in His presence can instantly change situations and cause improvements to come. Life is better because of Jesus.

Anyway, I had shared with him and the congregation at Calvary Lutheran that four weeks ago I prayed with a man named Ron whose hips and knees were supernaturally healed, but that this same man had his deaf ear opened last July when I prayed for him, and now he can hear great and walk without pain too. Even in that case, we specifically prayed for his hips to be healed, and God also healed his knee without us asking for that. Jesus is so cool. Praise God!

When I pray for healing, normally I just pray for about twenty to thirty seconds and then ask people to check their condition if they can, because we have learned that there is a miracle when you check. Recently, I was at a church in the Omaha area and was praying for people after the service. Several people were standing for prayer, and everyone who checked had at least seventy-five percent improvement, including one young fifteen-year-old girl who limped in with knee pain due to a fall while playing volleyball. Her knee was completely healed. Her mother, who was standing next to her, had stood for back pain. When I asked everyone to check, stating that there is a miracle when you check, she said out loud that she was not going to check, actually proclaiming that this was stupid. Her daughter was healed, as she started walking on it and checking it out, but the lady who said that this was stupid was the only one in the room who did not get well. She stood for the prayer but would not check.

Another lady at Calvary Lutheran came up to me in the morning and said all the arthritis in her thumbs seemed to have left. In the evening when she returned, she told me her thumbs had not hurt all afternoon and were still pain-free.

I later recalled and shared a time when at a local church called Lighthouse on the Hill, I had prayed for a lady with knee pain. As I did this, she fell to the floor under the power of the Holy Spirit and kind of yelled as she fell. She was in her seventies, and she lay on the floor for a long time, just enjoying the power of the Holy Spirit. (If you want to know more about this manifestation of falling under the power of God, you can read about it in my book *Willing to Yield*.)

Later, I saw her get up, limp out of the building, and limp out to her car, but in the evening when she came back in, she was walking as normal as could be. She told me that while on the floor, God reminded her of many people she needed to forgive, so she began to forgive everyone God brought to mind. After participating with God in this, she got up and then went home, ate lunch, took a nap, got up one hour later, and all her knee pain was gone. She also shared that we probably did not notice, but she had been wearing maternity clothes because she was severely bloated and had been that way for many weeks, and even though we only prayed for the knee, the bloating went away too. God is amazing! He is so caring and understanding.

A Good Testimony

At an Open Bible church in Des Moines, as I was explaining how the healing prayer would happen that evening, a man in the third row jumped up and began running around the church as he got well, just through the explanation, which included some testimonies. So we see again that the testimony of Jesus releases the spirit of prophecy (Rev. 19:10). First Corinthians 1:4–7 tells us that the testimony of Jesus enables us not to come up short in any area. In other words, God desires that nothing be lacking. In Hebrews 11:1–2, we know that faith is the substance of things hoped for and the evidence of things not seen, and by it, the elders obtained a good testimony. A good testimony is built on faith. What is a good testimony? One that advances the Kingdom and gives praise and honor to God.

There are several places in Psalm 119 where it speaks about the testimony of God, two of which talk about how those testimonies improve our soul. From 3 John we learn that God wants us to prosper and be in health, even as our soul prospers. Some people don't get well because their souls are not prospering. One way that people's souls don't prosper is, when they hear a testimony from others, they begin to complain to God and question why the other person got touched but they didn't. Not only don't they rejoice with the person who is sharing it, but they get mad at God and others because they are not experiencing the same power and healing released in their situation. If they would only apply the testimony of Jesus as the spirit of prophecy, and receive that testimony as a word of knowledge for them, then they could receive greater impact and possible healing so much more quickly.

We continue to see the miraculous and the power of God working in and through so many people, whether in students, churches, and yes, even businesses and the marketplace. All my books demonstrate, highlight, and teach many of these same themes and have wonderful heart-warming stories just like this one. It is intentional, as I want you to read the testimonies and believe that what God did for all these other people He can also do for you. Many people consistently tell me that, while reading my books, they feel like I am right there in the room, sharing with them. I hope that is true for you right now too. Well? Just kidding!

Eleventh Checkup: Unusual and Uncommon Un-Methods

Electronic Healing

Recently I was retelling about the time we offered a Facebook healing service. We set it up in advance and had several friends helping to pray for those who wrote in. We also asked everyone to get Spotify, so we had people from many countries around the world listening to the same praise and worship music together. Some people were so far away that it was actually the next day as we prayed for them across the International Dateline. Think about that. We prayed today, and the people were healed tomorrow at the very same time that it was today. We ended up hearing from over sixty people who were healed simply through writing out prayers on Facebook. We just prayed over each request, wrote out our prayers, and laid our hands on the computer before we sent them out, and asked God to deliver healing to each person.

I have had the opportunity on several occasions to use Skype for healing purposes. Some have just been between me and one other person, while others were for whole churches in third world nations. I wish I could show you some of the pictures and have you read some of the testimonies from these people in these countries, but even doing that could put the leaders and pastors of these churches at risk of physical harm and even death.

On one occasion, a friend named Mark Dommel sent me a text and asked for prayer for the pain in his back, so I wrote out a prayer and texted it back to him. Mark read it out loud, and within a very short amount of time, the back pain was completely gone. God is so awesome, and He walks right into our technology today and still performs mighty miracles and powerful healings.

So, I have been blessed to see so many healings happen so rapidly and quickly now. The prayers are generally pretty short, the power is generally pretty strong, and the results are amazing. In fact, it is so amazing that I love to watch people's expressions change. Often as I pray for groups of people, I see looks of wonder and hope, but suddenly when smiles start to appear, I know God is working. I don't have to wait for their hands to go up to tell me that something different is happening; I just look at their faces and see the glow and know that God has done something special. As I then ask them what is happening, they are so eager to share. This has been my experience: People who get well physically are the best advertisements for the Kingdom, as they readily want to share what happened. I believe healing services are great evangelistic tools. Anything that points to Jesus as the Savior is a good option.

Follow Jesus, not Methods

One of the reasons I used a made-up word ("un-methods") for the title of this chapter is because I am so against religious methods. Many in the church just love to do it exactly like some other anointed person, but the only person I want to follow and copy is Jesus. Years ago, when a certain televangelist was throwing his coat, others began to throw their coats. Some who have a great anointing wear certain clothes, so then others copy that style of dress, thinking that the anointing is in the look and appearance. I have seen the extremes of this, from really fancy formal dress to casual Hawaiian shirts and flip flops. Why do so many believers think that they have to copy someone else to be anointed or successful? Everyone is born an original, but most die as a copy. Just be you, and do it God's way, as He is working in you.

For a season, there was a young healing evangelist who would often say things like "BAM" or "Shamma" or some other crazy words, so others did the same when they got home and prayed for people. Some even closed out their letters or emails with those words. How silly and how ridiculous! Let's go after the authentic and the real and skip the hype that so often is around those trying to copy others. What a joke. Jesus often confronted the religious crowds of His day due to their insistence on following certain methods without having a heart relationship with the Lord. It is so easy to get caught up in that trap of doing something the same over and over simply because it worked before. You know the seven most deadly words in any church are: "We've always done it this way before" or "We've never done it this way before." How about, "Jesus is doing it this way, so I will too"? John

Eleventh Checkup: Unusual and Uncommon Un-Methods

Wimber was once approached and asked the question, "What do you do to get ready for a healing service?" His response was, "I drink a Diet Coke." I'm sure glad that I don't even like Diet Coke!

Once when I was a pastor in Kansas, we had a lady visit our church, specifically seeking healing, as we were known in that rural town as the ones who prayed and believed for healing. She had a huge blood sugar problem, and while praying for her, I had a word from the Lord that she should go off caffeine. Well, six weeks later, she returned to inform us that her blood sugars were normal and that she had taken my advice, and it wasn't hard. I had no idea what she was about to say, but she told us how each morning she had several cups of coffee, then switched to Cokes in the afternoon, often interchanged with Dr. Pepper and Mountain Dew, then in the evenings she would switch back to coffees and specialty coffee drinks. But she was able to go off all those products without any side effects at all, including headaches, which is something most people do have when they drop caffeine from their diets. Anyway, she just came by to tell us she was healed and to thank us for our prayers and our time.

One of my favorite "strange" healing testimonies that I enjoy sharing is about a lady in Ohio who had chronic back pain. After praying for her, I encouraged her to eat bananas, so after a couple days, she went to the store and purchased and then ate two bananas, as I had stated to eat bananas not just one. Though she felt foolish just going through the grocery checkout line with those two items, she did it, and afterwards her chronic back pain of many years vanished and never returned. She later inquired of me what caused that to happen, and I simply responded that I was obedient to share it with her and she was obedient to respond. God honors obedience in our lives, as well as faithfulness. We are stewards of His Kingdom, and 1 Corinthians 4:2 says that the requirement of stewards if to be found faithful. Proverbs 28:20 adds that a man who is found to be faithful will abound with many blessings.

There are times when I am simply driving down the road and I may get a headache or have a pain somewhere that just manifests. I will practice the words of Mark 16 and lay my hand on that pain, asking for God's presence and rebuking the pain or speaking healing, and the healing will manifest. I know what you are thinking, but while I am praying, I don't take both hands off of the steering wheel, only one. (smile)

As you know from a previous chapter, we have just launched out and planted a new church called Kingdom Encounters. One of our values is that we embrace what Jesus is doing, not what He is not doing. There is a difference and a distinction, but to know what it is, you must remain close to the Lord so that you know where He is going, what He is doing, and how He is going to approach the situation. If you do that, your soul will prosper, and I believe you will be in health. Only the naysayers who can't figure out why you are so successful, so prosperous, and so blessed will respond, "Well, well, well."

Twelfth Checkup
Eating Disorderly

Just as I finished writing this chapter, a diet joke arrived in my email, so I thought I would share it here as a funny prelude:

Weight Loss Hotline

Thank you for calling the Weight Loss Hotline.

If you'd like to lose a half pound right now, press "1" 18,000 times.

For approximately fifteen years, I traveled in full-time ministry and spent a lot of time on airplanes, in hotels, and doing ministry at over 1700 churches, schools, and businesses around the nation. In many ways, I loved it because I got to meet so many new and interesting people around the country and even in other parts of the world. Plus I was able to see many new locations and interesting sights that I would have probably never seen otherwise. Some of those include Sandpoint, Idaho; Ely, Minnesota; Gadsden, Alabama; West Palm Beach, Florida; Virginia Beach, Virginia; Boston, Massachusetts; Washington, D.C.; and yes, even Honolulu, Hawaii, two times.

But it was during this time that I began to develop some bad eating and exercise habits, or perhaps I should say lack of exercise habits. Mostly, it was the eating that was contributing to my continued weight gain. I am not blaming the traveling on this; although, that certainly was a contributing factor. I am responsible for my own personal wellbeing, and I take ownership of my own shortcomings, submitting them to God in prayer for future help in overcoming difficulties and situations to which I have opened the door. It was often very easy to go through church pot blessing lines and load up my plate with all sorts of unhealthy foods and snacks, whether during morning brunch times or lunch, and specifically at restaurants where pastors often took me to eat. The evening meals that could happen anywhere from nine to midnight after those evening services were the worst.

As I began to put on more and more weight, I had to eat more during the week when I was at home to keep up with what I was doing on the weekend, which then contributed to my wife Diane gaining weight too. As a result, my heart rate and blood pressure, along with my cholesterol levels, began to accelerate up beyond the borderline normal range. My knees, legs, and ankles, along with even my shoulders and neck, began to hurt so much more too. This led to more and more doctor and chiropractor visits, as well as taking more over the counter and sometimes prescription-strength pain meds to help me just get by.

Eating to Live

While I was bringing life to many others, I was actually slowly bringing death to various parts of my body through this food abuse I now call "eating disorderly." It wasn't a disorder like other eating maladies, but it definitely was the sin of gluttony, and I needed to repent and get right with God in this area of my life.

In 2013, while driving home to Omaha eastbound on Interstate 80 from North Platte, Nebraska, I stopped at a rest area near Grand Island, Nebraska, and prayed one of those short, one-sentence prayers that went like this: "God, I need help." That was it. I just sat in my car and thought about my prayer when suddenly I heard the Lord speak to me.

He was kind and not condemning in any way. He simply said that He had an eating plan for Diane and me and that, if we followed it for eight months, we would lose weight and it would become a lifestyle for us. Then He began to share the plan, and I wrote it all down as quickly as I could. I actually started the plan that day by purchasing a healthy vegetable smoothie for lunch and another one for dinner, rather than my normal fast food stops that I was accustomed to making on driving trips. Yes, you read that

Twelfth Checkup: Eating Disorderly

correctly: a vegetable smoothie. I bought them at a Wal-Mart. I can feel your eyes rolling already, but read on.

I took the eating plan home to Diane, and we decided to give it a try. We also shared it with our son Jason, who was in great shape, and asked him to pray for us. He later confided in me that while he was praying, he initially had his doubts that this might work, as we had tried several times to lose weight and had a measure of success each time, but then put the same weight back on. But somehow, I knew in my spirit that this time would be different because we had a heaven-made plan just for us.

There were days and weeks that we made lots of progress, and then there were weeks when we would plateau and not make any progress at all, but we kept going. Each morning we would weigh ourselves and then pray for each other as well. Keep in mind that we started this eating plan in September, which was leading into three major fall and winter holidays, plus lots of holiday parties and my birthday and Jason's birthday too. But we kept going.

And we made good decisions along the way. For instance, last Christmas Diane did not do any holiday baking at all. No traditional cookies, no family recipes for pies and cakes, and only one glass of eggnog consumed the whole season. That in and of itself was a miracle and proved that God was in this. For Thanksgiving and Christmas, we had the exact same dessert: baked apples with some cool whip on them. Not only was it healthy, but there were no tempting leftovers to munch on for several days. And yes, we both lost weight during those two seasons.

As I write this chapter, it is December 2014, and we have been maintaining this eating plan now for fifteen months. At the one year mark, we had lost 130 pounds between us, as I was down 72 pounds and Diane was down 58 pounds. Diane lost six dress sizes, and I lost ten pants sizes. We gave away bags and bags of clothing, mostly to those on the street but also to other donation centers. My heart rate, blood pressure, and cholesterol returned to normal, and our overall health greatly improved. Diane had fun buying and wearing dresses again—even some high heels, which she had not worn in years. She commented that she turned into a young lady again. After she lost the weight, she now looks at least twenty years younger than her real age. One of our dear friends, Barbara Crider, who wrote the opening prayer for my second book, *Willing to Yield*, often refers to us as the incredible shrinking couple. If you would like to see a progression of pictures through the whole eating process, you can find those located on my Facebook page.

Prior to this eating plan, I actually had tried several diets; but none of them really worked for me, and in one case I was on two diets at once. Yeah, I could not get enough to eat on just one diet (smile). But the real reason that diets just did not work for me was that I just had too much on my plate. Okay, enough already!

My beginning weight was 299 pounds, and my goal was to get below 235 pounds, and now I stay around the 227 to 230 range. I thought about going to 220, which is what I weighed in high school, but I later recognized that my motive for doing that was vanity, and that would be the wrong reason for sure. I am 6'7" tall, so 235 is the ideal weight, according to the medical charts. Diane and I each weigh less than we did when we got married in 1979, so that in and of itself is definitely an achievement. God helped us every step of the way, and we now do appreciate and understand that the steps of the righteous truly are ordered of the Lord. We are so grateful for His help and His plan, which I will share in just a bit.

I want to add that we did not change our exercise routines at all, but just our eating habits. And I am going to share this one point now: Not eating after 7 p.m. is crucial to being successful. Now, I know what you are thinking, because so many people start to get hungry around 8 or 9 at night and then just end up eating way too much food for their bodies to digest properly overnight. But this really is a big key to the plan.

Let me be honest: Many nights, even to this day, I start to get hungry around 9 p.m. or so, but when that happens, I first remind myself that I am going to go to sleep around 11 p.m. and be getting up at 6:15, or some days even earlier, so surely I can make it until I go to bed. But if the food cravings continue, I pray and ask God for assistance with the fruit of the Spirit of self-control.

Twelfth Checkup: Eating Disorderly

That is a big one for most believers. The reality is that if I can't practice self-control for two hours, I am not nearly as mature as I should be for a believer who has been walking with Jesus now for nearly forty-five years.

So here is the plan as it was given to me by the Lord. I hope it is helpful to you, but if you should decide to adopt it as a lifestyle change, then please consult your doctor before launching out into this. Keep in mind there are hundreds of diet books that you can purchase. This is not a diet, but an eating plan, and we believe that it was specifically given to us, as God knew the makeup of our bodies, and our metabolism. While we are fearfully and wonderfully made just like you, the plan He has for you might look a lot different from the one He gave us.

Eating Orderly

On September 21, 2013, God literally downloaded this eating plan to me at a rest area along Interstate 80 in Nebraska.

We only eat salads, soup, fish, and chicken, or non-meat dinners during the weekday nights. As I stated before, we try not to eat after 7 p.m. each night, but there are exceptions when invited to eat with someone else or say at a wedding reception, etc.

We cut out white potatoes, pasta, bread, and sweets at night and switched to organic fruits, veggies, and dairy. Also, we use unsalted butter and lots of coconut oil, and we drink lots of water and now filter our own water, also making our own unsweetened iced tea. We do still drink coffee in the morning and occasionally in the evening, but we switched from using all sorts of flavored creams in regular coffee and now drink flavored coffee with less regular cream and less sweetened creamers.

Diane and I have what we want for breakfast and lunch, just smaller portions. Breakfast can be cereal, oatmeal, eggs, and even waffles and pancakes occasionally. We moved away from high fructose corn syrup and sometimes just use honey or raw honey. We also eat lots of Greek yogurt, and we switched to flat bread for sandwiches. That was hard for me, as I am a lover of breads, for sure.

Normally, we only eat red meat once or twice a week, usually on weekends. Each time we eat salad, we look for ways to change up the salads and do them differently. Now we only buy juices and smoothies that are made fresh, nothing from concentrate, and if there is any sugar in them, it is way down the list of ingredients. Yes, we have snacks during the day, which could be yogurt, banana bread, fruit, snack bars, nuts, and raisins. I buy primarily organic fruit, vegetables, and other products such as dairy, cereals, soups and so on. Yes, organic is more expensive than non-organic, but I think the tradeoff is worth it for us to be healthier. Besides, if we were to add up the many pies, cakes, cookies, ice-cream, and other similar types of foods that we no longer purchase, I would guess that we are breaking even.

Fast food restaurants are off limits unless we plan to get a salad or perhaps an iced tea. We don't do soda at all. This one was easier for me, as I went off of soda about twelve years ago.

As I stated above, we pray for each other every morning and weigh ourselves every morning too. Our exercise has not changed much; although, in the warmer months, we do walk more and of course work in our yard.

When eating out, we will make good choices, such as asking for dressing on the side of a salad, requesting no chips with a sandwich at Subway or Panera, etc., and often going for the low-calorie meals. I wrote above about some of our sweet substitutes for special holidays, and we continue that trend even this year after we have achieved our goals.

I did mention that last year I had only one small glass of eggnog whereas usually I have several quarts. I know, I need eggnog deliverance. Pray for me! Prior to going off soda, I used to mix eggnog with Sprite, and if you want a really delicious drink, try blending it with peppermint ice-cream. That's probably not what you want to hear right now, but I really do enjoy Texas Toast dipped in vanilla eggnog and fried up with fresh strawberries on top, but that is only once a year now; whereas in the past it was several times from the end of October through January. Sometimes, we still have it on the Fourth of July because eggnog freezes just fine in those quart containers. It's implied, but I am an

Twelfth Checkup: Eating Disorderly

eggnog junkie now practicing the Holy Spirit fruit of self-control, so that is the primary fruit I now enjoy. And I truly mean *enjoy*. The fruit of the Spirit is great fruit and will add tremendous value to your life. We all need the gifts of the Spirit coupled with the fruit of the Spirit. The gifts of the Spirit release the ministry of Jesus, and the fruit of the Spirit release the character of Jesus.

To this day, we continue to make tough choices, but we also celebrate. On our thirty-fifth wedding anniversary in August of 2014, Diane and I went to the Cheesecake Factory. We had low-calorie meals, but then we both had huge pieces of specialty cheesecake. Believe it or not, that next morning, we were down two pounds each. However, we went for a long walk after dinner, and we started that morning by playing basketball together at our local health club. It was kind of funny, actually, when we told Jason that his fifty-seven-year-old parents were going out to play basketball together, but our weight loss has enabled us to now be able to run and do laps and layups. Just don't ask me, though, if the ball ever went in the hoop. While I am happy to be able to play sports again, I am equally glad no one was filming us, either!

I asked God if we could have treat nights when we reached certain goals, and He said we could as a reward but then had to return to the plan the next day. We continue to follow this now as well. I do have water bottles in the car, by my bed, in my office, and in other places to remind to drink more water. I am so hydrated now that I often don't drink anything with my meals. Interestingly enough, when I was overweight, I would drink coffee or soda before going to sleep and then would have to use the restroom once or twice in the middle of the night, but now I can drink water before I go to sleep and often sleep through the entire night without the urge to get up. It is really amazing.

Even though God did not specifically give me any exercise notes, I have made choices that have assisted the process. For instance, in hotels I will not use the elevator except when checking in or out; otherwise, I walk the stairs. And in airports, regardless of the time between flights, I walk the terminal, rarely sitting down. I also skip the coffees, lattes, and other unhealthy airport food. When I go to stores and shopping centers, I often park farther away and walk from a distance into the store and back. Sometimes, I also pick up a few carts and return them to the cart stalls.

I do various exercise bursts during the day, usually five to ten minutes at a time, (depending on my location and how I feel), just doing different exercises for ten minutes or so, then back to the task I was working on. Even when waking up in the morning, I will do some leg lifts or various types of leg movements to generate some exercise before arising for the day.

So there you have it: our eating plan that has returned us to God's plan for our lives. We are in the process of being restored and regaining some of the health we lost due to our own foolish sinful desires. But God is One Who can indeed change, transform, and restore us, and I believe He can do it for you too.

In closing I am going to share a food testimony that is a bit different. One time about two years ago, I was invited to speak to a highly multicultural youth group. While walking in the door, the Lord spoke to me and said that I was to offer to pray for those who had eating disorders, that there would be five who would respond, and two of them would be guys.

This was a pretty radical revelation, and I wanted to be sure I was hearing God correctly, so I immediately asked for a Scripture verse to somehow relate to this prophetic word. The Lord had me turn to Ezekiel 3:1–3, and this is what I read:

> Moreover He said to me, "Son of man, eat what you find; eat this scroll, and go, speak to the house of Israel." So I opened my mouth, and He caused me to eat that scroll.
>
> And He said to me, "Son of man, feed your belly, and fill your stomach with this scroll that I give you." So I ate, and it was in my mouth like honey in sweetness.

I immediately had courage to go in and share this word. Right at the conclusion of my message, I gave the word that there were five people there with eating disorders and that two of them

Twelfth Checkup: Eating Disorderly

were guys. That is exactly who responded: three young ladies and two young men. I used a method, though, that I frequently use for more private introspection when dealing with certain issues. I had everyone close their eyes and bow their heads and then asked for those who felt they were the ones to just look at me with their eyes, and then I would know for whom I was to pray. But afterwards, I then asked if they felt courageous enough to stand for prayer—that no one would look down upon them—and all five of them stood up. It was a very precious moment, as their friends gathered around them to offer prayer and support.

God may be talking to you right now about some of your eating habits. Maybe like me, you have been eating disorderly, or perhaps you just overindulge in one area that is unhealthy for you. I know that God wants the very best for you and that He loves you just as much as He loves me. If you sense that God is asking you to trust Him and to step out in faith with a new plan, just go to Him now in prayer. You can trust Him for sure. Get into His Word and allow the Word to get into you. Yes, that may even mean eating the scroll, which would be a good thing too. Whatever He asks you to do, respond in faith and begin to make lifestyle changes. When you get to your promised land, you too will undoubtedly have an amazing testimony.

Taste and see that the Lord is good.

Thirteenth Checkup
Wells, Shacks, and Cisterns

There are lots of stories in the Bible dealing with wells, so I decided to include one of them here near the end of this book. In this chapter I am blending some notes from my former pastor and now my overseer, Pastor Jim Hart of Eagle's Nest Worship Center, with some of my own thoughts about a New Testament well experience with Jesus and the Samaritan woman. There are some interesting insights that will be helpful to you as you work toward concluding this particular book. So let's read the story below and then continue with the teaching and sharing that will follow.

The Well Is Deep

> Now Jacob's well was there. Jesus therefore, being wearied from His journey, sat thus by the well. It was about the sixth hour. A woman of Samaria came to draw water. Jesus said to her, "Give Me a drink." For His disciples had gone away into the city to buy food.

> Then the woman of Samaria said to Him, "How is it that You, being a Jew, ask a drink from me, a Samaritan [watch station; to hedge about (as with thorns), that is, guard; generally to protect, attend to] woman?" For Jews have no dealings with Samaritans.

Jesus answered and said to her, "If you knew the gift of God, and who it is who says to you, 'Give Me a drink,' you would have asked Him, and He would have given you living water."

The woman said to Him, "Sir, You have nothing to draw with, and the well is deep. Where then do You get that living water? Are You greater than our father Jacob, who gave us the well, and drank from it himself, as well as his sons and his livestock?"

Jesus answered and said to her, "Whoever drinks of this water will thirst again, but whoever drinks of the water that I shall give him will never thirst. But the water that I shall give him will become in him a fountain of water springing up into everlasting life."

The woman said to Him, "Sir, give me this water, that I may not thirst, nor come here to draw."

Jesus said to her, "Go, call your husband, and come here."

The woman answered and said, "I have no husband."

Jesus said to her, "You have well said, 'I have no husband,' for you have had five husbands, and the one whom you now have is not your husband; in that you spoke truly."

The woman said to Him, "Sir, I perceive that You are a prophet. Our fathers worshiped on this mountain [Refers to Mt. Gerizim, on which the

Thirteenth Checkup: Wells, Shacks, and Cisterns

Samaritans built a temple as a rival place of worship, since they were not welcome in the Jerusalem temple] and you Jews say that in Jerusalem is the place where one ought to worship."

Jesus said to her, "Woman, believe Me, the hour is coming when you will neither on this mountain, nor in Jerusalem, worship the Father. You worship what you do not know; we know what we worship, for salvation is of the Jews. But the hour is coming, and now is, when the true worshipers will worship the Father in spirit and truth; for the Father is seeking such to worship Him. God is Spirit, and those who worship Him must worship in spirit and truth." (John 4:6–24, notes added)

Here, the woman represents the church. She should have been in a place of maturity and meeting others' needs instead of having to have her needs met. This is because she has lost her relationship and dependency on and in Christ. There are many people in the Kingdom who forsake their dependency on Jesus, in search of other things that they are attracted to. Sometimes these are sin issues, and other times they are just something that has its appeal but over time drains the life of Jesus from a prominent place to one that is relegated to Christmas and Easter and delegated to times of great need.

Sometimes I hear pastors respond to those returning to a church after being absent for a long time with the condescending tone of "Well, well, well, look who finally came back to church." But I don't believe you will ever hear Jesus respond that way if you ever have to return to Him. He will certainly respond to you as the father who runs to meet his lost child does in the story of the prodigal son.

Jesus knows full well what is going on with this woman, but His responses are awesome, in that He is endeavoring to teach and train while simultaneously being kind and generous with His time and His words. Not only does Jesus know full well what is happening, but His desire is that her spiritual life be a full well of God, with influencing living water that will never run dry, never run out, and never run away. Jesus is Immanuel, God with us, and His character, presence, and gifts and callings remain with us too. To know the character of God is to know God. I am confident that if God wanted to, He could look at any of us and state, "What a character." But He sees the character of Jesus in us and responds, "There is my son. There is my daughter. Those are my kids! I love them."

Five Senses

This woman had five husbands. These represent our five natural senses and trying to live a spiritual life through our own natural wisdom. The senses are: (1) sight, (2) hearing, (3) smell, (4) touch, and (5) taste. When we try to live merely through our human understanding, we wear ourselves out.

The church frequently does this too, relying on market-tested methods and experiences that they can see rather than relying in faith on the Lord's plan, which has perhaps not been revealed yet. And that contributes to personal and pastoral burnout and congregations often living off natural stagnant water rather than the spiritual living water. This then erodes more and more faith from those in the pews as the spiritual water supply runs dry, and people end up walking (or in some cases, running) away from the faith. At the very least, they get disenfranchised from church in general. I mentioned in a previous chapter about pastors, leaders, and those in the pews often imitating the antics or behavior, sometimes even parroting the speech of certain leaders, thinking that the anointing is in the words, the style of dress, or the delivery.

Thirteenth Checkup: Wells, Shacks, and Cisterns

In reality, the anointing is in the Holy Spirit Who is encased within that individual.

Like the Pharisees, it often becomes more of a spectacle about what can be seen rather than what is not seen. Faith in God responds to the unseen realm and takes precedence over the seen. This Samaritan woman has ceased to draw on the wells of living water by the Spirit and is now trying to use natural means: "You have nothing to draw with." What she doesn't recognize is that the conversation with Jesus Himself is actually drawing her into the realm of the Spirit and when applied, she becomes the bucket to draw the water. We are all buckets who need to be filled with the living water of Jesus.

Without Jesus, all you have is a religious exercise and form and ritual; but with Jesus, you have an encounter that enables you to experience something far greater than any religion has to offer. Jesus, Who would never with a condescending tone respond, "Well, well, well," but with a bright note of optimism, looks at us and sees us healthy, prosperous, full of wisdom, and in a state of wellness. As we partake of that living water, we taste the new wine of the Spirit. The water now turned into wine once again is the best tasting wine that has an eternal value, longevity, and vintage to it that makes it remarkable. If you have a relationship with Jesus, that's you.

The sixth man the Samaritan woman isn't even married to, just living with. And six is the number of man. In Genesis we learn that man was created on the sixth day, and in Revelation 13:18 we discover that the number of the beast is from the number of man, adding it to be 666. Now, she is just shacking up, trying to use the wisdom and systems of the world to satisfy, but nothing does; not herself or the world or this sixth man.

Shacks

Psalm 127:1–2 says:

> If GOD doesn't build the house, the builders only build shacks. If GOD doesn't guard the city, the night watchman might as well nap. It's useless to rise early and go to bed late, and work your worried fingers to the bone. Don't you know he enjoys giving rest to those he loves?

And Proverbs 14:11 declares, "Lives of careless wrongdoing are tumbledown shacks; holy living builds soaring cathedrals."

Both of these Scriptures from the Message Bible imply that any house without God as the center is descriptive of a shack. When I did a word study on the word *shack*, I discovered that when it is extended out, it becomes the word *shackled*. Without God, we are literally shackled to the enemy and the world's ways of doing things, but if and only if we trust in Jesus and the power of His Holy Spirit, will we then experience true liberty and freedom.

Ecclesiastes 10:18 (MSG) adds still another component with these piercing words: "A shiftless man lives in a tumbledown shack; a lazy woman ends up with a leaky roof." So the roof of the shack begins to leak. Either way, you are going to experience water in some form: living water through the wells of Jesus that can repair, restore, and bring a life of celebration, or leaking water making a mess of everything that it touches.

This clearly comes into focus when she has a revelation of Christ (the seventh Man—seven is the number of completion and perfection) and that He and He alone is her true husband. Only He brings completion. The other six are gone and in the past, so she is encouraged as are you to now focus on the newness and the wellness of simply knowing and walking with Jesus. Some think that it is hard to grasp, but in reality it is one of the easiest things you will ever do.

True satisfaction and hope for today and the future only come in Christ Jesus!

With that thought I would like to share a letter that my friend Shane Rootes posted on Facebook in December of 2014. Shane is a good friend and a talented, anointed, and gifted worship leader that we met at a local church here in Omaha. His words penned below will add significance to the statement from Pastor Jim Hart that true satisfaction and hope for today and the future only come in Christ Jesus.

Expression by Impression

The Expression of Christ is revealed through an impression of Christ.

It's a week since I was in the hospital. I am slowly getting my strength back. The viral infection is still strong, and the pain at times intense. I am so very thankful for the love and care shown to me and my family, by doctors, nurses, family, and friends from all over the world. From artists, musicians, endorsement company and music industry icons.

Thank you for praying, interceding for us and lifting us up before the Lord.

It will be another week or two before I see the neurologist to assess the pending surgery. We are praying that this tumor shrivels up and dies without the need for surgery.

On and off all week I have asked God, "Why?"

As I was praying, I sensed the Spirit speak these words: "The expression of Christ is revealed through an impression of Christ."

Impressions that leave a mark are painful. Think of an animal getting "branded" with a hot iron. The impression is painful, but from that point on everyone knew whom the animal belonged to.

James 1:2: "Be joyful when you face trials of many kinds." That is really easy to read and very hard to live out. However, in the midst of the pain of this last week, I've known and felt the presence of Jesus. It has left an impression on me which in turn will be an expression.

Whilst I don't like the sickness, I know it's an opportunity for me in the painful times to have Christ make an impression on me. The expression will be to other people who are suffering, who feel helpless or hopeless, expressing Jesus on the way.

When we allow Jesus to be with us in the good, the bad, and the nasty times, He will always leave an impression. Whether it is healing, the right word, comfort, peace, or hope, His impressions are lasting. Hosea encourages that they are "etched on the heart" of any man or woman who seeks the truth of who He is.

God did not cause this sickness. But in the process, the Jesus I love and serve will be glorified. The impression felt this last week will be an expression of Jesus.

Maybe today you are sick, down, or unhappy with life. Or you could be in the exact opposite place.

Thirteenth Checkup: Wells, Shacks, and Cisterns

Wherever you are in this life journey; be thankful for this moment. God is doing something in your life that allows an impression of Jesus to be made, which in turn will reveal itself as an expression of Christ.

Philippians 2 is one of my favorite passages of Scripture. It calls us to be "like minded," to be and act as Christ did. This is your moment and my moment to see the impression of Christ revealed through an expression of worship to someone who needs Jesus. In the midst of our crazy lives, we just need to allow Him to do that.

His body was desecrated with the impression of a falling world, my sin. But in the midst of this chaos, He does not come to chastise, to scold or scorn. He comes as Hope, Healer, and Life Giver, an impression that will result in an expression.

In the midst of life's crazy rollercoaster moments, we (I) need to stop and thank Him for the moment, however hard and painful. It's a divine opportunity to see His hand at work!

Broken Cisterns

In Jeremiah 2:13, we find these profound words: "For My people have committed two evils: They have forsaken Me, the fountain of living waters, and hewn themselves cisterns, broken cisterns that can hold no water." From Dictionary.com, we learn that a cistern is a reservoir, tank, or container for storing or holding water or other liquid.

Jesus made an impression on the woman at the well, and it happened through the expression of Jesus that my friend Shane wrote about. Our impressions of God are often shaped by life's courses and the many events in our lives. Some are positive, and some are less than positive, but all give us opportunities to draw on the waters of salvation. Isaiah 12:3 declares, "Therefore with joy you will draw water from the wells of salvation."

The dictionary definition of a cistern includes that of a reservoir, and I mention that because I have been teaching a series of messages at Kingdom Encounters titled, "Expanding Our Capacity for the Supernatural." The word *capacity* literally means "to hold and contain," just like a reservoir holds and contains water. But capacity also means "to release." Likewise, a reservoir, while it holds and contains large amounts of water, is also designed to release that water to the people for their personal use.

Two more examples would include a fire station and an airport. A fire station holds trucks, ladders, hoses, equipment, and first responders, but if these things are not released when you have an emergency, what good would that fire station really be? In the same way, an airport will hold baggage handlers, airplanes, luggage compartments, fuel for the planes, check-in counters, boarding gates, and so on. But if the planes are not released to fly and carry the passengers to their destination, all you have is a Hollywood movie with Tom Hanks as the star.

We are told in the Bible that we hold the Holy Spirit, but if we don't release the Holy Spirit to others, then we are not fulfilling the mandate of Jesus to go into all the world, which includes your local grocery store, post office, bank, school, and other places of business that you frequent and share the great news about Jesus.

You may remember from chapter one that the word *capacity* has an additional meaning. Let's refresh our memories. If we divide the word in half, that leaves us with "capa" and "city." A "city" is a place of commerce, education, marketplace, finance, and community. But "capa" is the red cape that the bull fighter uses to attract the bull. I don't mean to belittle anyone, but there has been enough attraction of religious bull for centuries, and it is time for us as believers to rise up and attract the Holy Spirit to our cities. Shout with me: NO MORE RELIGIOUS BULL!

The problem for many is that religion has shackled us to shacks that don't have the presence of the Lord flowing in and through them. In fact, many of them have leaking cisterns and dry

Thirteenth Checkup: Wells, Shacks, and Cisterns

wells due to all of the religious stuff that many try to label as the church today. It is time for a change, and you and I are the new change agents to get this accomplished. According to the passage above from Jeremiah, the church has forsaken Jesus and tried to make religious structures their waterways; but the waterways are cracked and leaking, containing poisonous water rather than living water from the well of salvation in Jesus Christ.

So my friend Shane is right: The expression of Jesus is revealed through the impression of Jesus. We already learned that intercession brings revelation, so that revealing process is ongoing and often happens through prayer. You can have that impression expression happen right now as well.

You may think that, with regards to Jesus, you have a shack mentality or that you are shackled to something that you just can't seem to get free from, but Jesus declared that He has come to give us life and life that is more abundant than anything else we have ever tried or experienced. The Bible tells us that it is the Spirit of God Who gives and brings freedom. I want to help you, if need be, to move from the swamp to the river and then to have wells and cisterns that are strong and won't break down and decay.

I want you to enjoy the presence of Jesus so much that with each day that passes, you can say to yourself, "Well, well, well, look at how Jesus is working in my life! What a difference I am now from what I used to be." You may have gone through multiple divorces, terrible heartache, several failed business ventures, and very tough health issues, but I am here to tell you that Jesus can take care of your past, make you a brand new "you" today, and promote you into a fantastic future if you will just trust Him and believe Him today.

Why don't you pray this simple prayer?

Dear Jesus, thank You for offering to share Your life with me. My life is kind of confusing right now, and I really could use Your help. Your Word says that You are a present help in a time of trouble, and I believe You always tell the truth. So Your Word is good enough for me because I do need your help. Would You come and help me right now? I invite You into my life. Fill me with life-giving water. I need You. I repent of all my sins and now believe that You are my Lord and Savior and my very best friend. Thank You, Jesus, for coming into my life. Please come live big in me so that I can live big for You. Thank You so very much. I pray this believing in You, trusting in You, and now loving You, knowing that You love me even more. Amen.

Fourteenth Checkup
Supernatural Perseverance

If you have not read the Preliminary Diagnosis at the beginning of this book, please go back and read it now. On occasion, I have told pastors that it sometimes takes more faith to stay in one location than it does to move to a new one. I also believe that sometimes it takes more faith to persevere through a less than positive ongoing situation than it does to believe for an instantaneous solution. According to 2 Peter 1:6, perseverance is sandwiched between self-control and godliness. Self-control is a fruit of the Spirit that God intends us to utilize in our lives. Godliness is an attribute of knowing Jesus. With self-control at the beginning and godliness at the end, we are able to persevere in the middle. But all three require supernatural power from the Lord.

This will undoubtedly be an unusual conclusion for you, but it is an honest one and in many ways should bring you hope, especially if you are personally persevering through some disease or ongoing medical affliction. Perhaps you have a good friend or relative who is in this situation too. My goal is to be authentic in my approach to healing and not have you discover this some other way and then leave shaking your head and muttering to yourself, "Well, well, well." Rather, I hope and pray that my free-flowing and formulated thoughts will convey truth, accuracy, and a dependence on God, just like you are presently doing for yourself or someone near you.

New Illness

Just after launching into the writing of this manuscript, I actually became somewhat ill myself; although, I did not recognize it. About six months ago, I began to have an intermittent sore throat that would come and go at various times during each day. Initially, it would only be there for ten to twenty minutes at a time and then be absent from me for several hours before returning. But over the summer months the extended durations of pain would be longer and longer, and my time without any pain was shortened considerably.

We gradually went to pray with friends and those who believe in the power of healing. I began to see my doctor, and a variety of medicines for a possible cure were tried, but none of them worked. These included allergy meds, antibiotics, shots, and some other medical guesses that I don't recall presently. Finally, based on the symptoms and when they would occur, it was determined that I most likely was battling GERD or Acid Reflux, which was sending this up to my throat and then lodging there. So as I write this conclusion, I have been battling a pretty constant sore throat now for six months. At times it is just scratchy and slightly sore, sometimes affecting my palate too, while at other times feeling like I have strep throat.

I frequently get prayer every day from family and friends, plus I take a prescription to help calm it, along with probiotics and a few other remedies that others have tried with success. My progress is slow, but nonetheless, it is progress. It seems that I often experience great breakthroughs when praying for others, yet with myself, it frequently takes a longer time span to accomplish the same result. I am unsure why this is; although I have had many others share their impressions of this. Still, it remains a mystery to me. However, even in the toughest times personally, God gives me strength, assurance, faith, and tenacity actually to continue to pray for others and see awesome healings. Some of the healing stories you read about in this book were actually prayed for while I was also battling this acid reflux. That is a mystery, for sure. Simultaneously, I am always very grateful when anyone gets well.

Yet, while I battle this in my own life, I try to stay focused on what God is doing and not on what He is not doing. In other words, I understand timing and desire to be in the center of His will, so I just do what I see Him doing regarding myself and others. If I sense I am to pray a certain way by and through His leading, then I go that direction. If I believe I am to say no to the prescriptions or probiotics on a certain day, I respond in faith, even

Fourteenth Checkup: Supernatural Perseverance

though I may be emotionally battling this and wondering what is actually happening. I know that some of you have been in that situation too. You want to please God and walk in faith and at the same time you spend time contemplating the whole situation with bewilderment at how quickly others seem to get well, and yet you or your friends are not. That is exactly the position I have found myself in at various times. I have even had a few days of deeper discouragement, and it was at those times that the prayers of my family, namely my wife Diane and our son Jason, along with closer friends, carried me through to the next day with their prayers.

Bearing Burdens

Galatians 6:2 speaks of bearing one another's burdens, and the scene is one of a stake being driven in to hold up a tomato plant so that the fruit of the vine does not drag on the ground and become useless through decay. I have on occasion been the recipient of a burden-bearing stake and rope to appropriately tie me to someone else for a season of personal spiritual care that could only happen through the love and grace of Jesus. Any other way would have been futile, but with Jesus, all things are possible.

I am believing that I will be well soon, perhaps even before this book is published, but it is possible that this book could be out there for a year or more before I am healed of this infirmity. I believe it is in Psalm 34:19 where it says that many are the afflictions of the righteous, but the Lord delivers us out of them all. When I had Irritable Bowel Syndrome, it took three years. With skin cancer in my ear, it took five years. The neck and shoulder pain lasted for over twenty years. But the reoccurring wart on my elbow was supernaturally healed in two months, and the bone spur in my foot was touched by God in two days.

I won't speculate about the reasons for some things taking so much longer than others, but I will authenticate once again that Jesus is Lord, and He wants you and me to be healthy and well. In reality, I believe He is more invested in our healing than we are. I know for a truthful fact that according to Romans 8:34, He is at the right hand of the Father praying for us even right now as you read this final chapter. It's His nature and so much a part of His character to do this. His manifested life goals remain the same because not only does He love us, but He is love, and His love is from everlasting to everlasting. Simplifying, it is definitely eternal. My trust and hope is secure in Him, and I believe I will soon be well.

Let me also add that it is okay to be honest in your personal appraisals when people ask how you are feeling, especially when battling something significant, whether that is healing, a financial attack, or a relationship issue. I have met some folks who teach that you should never say anything that sounds remotely negative or even gives a hint that you are speaking more about the pain of the suffering, rather than faith in what He can do for you and me. But I don't find this to be a real or good representation of Scripture.

I see many places in the Bible where the Bible characters who were being written about shared their real emotions and their sincere feelings in the midst of certain tragedies and very difficult circumstances. There is a tendency by some theological persuasions not to say anything that does not have faith statements built in like a fortress, without calling attention to the obvious cracks in the mortar holding the bricks in place in that fortress. What I mean is that some will say never to tell anyone that you are hurting or that you are in pain, but to ignore it and always respond with strong words of faith that make the hearer think you are some super human who somehow is able to bypass the pain and just be something that you are not.

I would prefer to be practical rather than pretentious. When I was sick with IBS and people would ask me how I was feeling, I would often describe the painful symptoms or share how good or bad the night before might have been, but then I would also add in a Scripture verse or a biblical declaration of what I was believing for God to do. This way, I felt like I was being honest. To me, denying the symptoms is being dishonest, and dishonesty is a lie, and a lie is a sin. This may or may not be an undeniable fact, but I am sticking with it anyway.

Fourteenth Checkup: Supernatural Perseverance

Discouraged Response

The story of the man who was at the pool of Bethesda in John 5 is a great example of this because, as Jesus entered the area, He encountered this man, who the Bible says had been there a long time. Jesus asked Him if he wanted to get well. The man responded that, due to his condition, he could not move into the water when the supernatural movement happened because he did not have a helper or an aid to assist him. So I want you to catch this. Jesus asked the man if he wanted to get well, and the man did not answer the question but gave a very discouraged response as to why he couldn't get well.

There was no evidence of any faith in this story, but only gut-wrenching real drama that this man was facing on a daily basis as people around him got well every single day while he was left out. Not only was he left out, but he was left stranded there to watch others get well and only be able to wish that he could also experience the elation and euphoria of such a glorious encounter with God.

And Jesus healed him anyway.

I want that to sink in. Jesus healed him anyway.

No faith declaration. No Scripture verse to stand on and memorize. No praying in the Spirit for wisdom, understanding, and discernment. No anointing with oil for healing. Just an apparent complaining, discontented, almost resentful response, as if to seek sympathy from the question, "Do you want to be made well?"

I am not discounting faith at all because the majority of the healing passages in Scripture do have a faith component, but I also believe that Jesus understands our frailty, and He still offers to come to us and touch us even at times and during seasons when after standing or waiting for a long time, we find ourselves totally discouraged, frustrated, and perhaps even depressed. And then, in the midst of the worst part of the storm, there He is walking on the waves of the sea, right toward us. Yes, He can still catch a wave today just like He did in the biblical narratives. And He doesn't have to go through the surfing ritual that my brother Jim shared in the first chapter, but instead He actually knows the wind and the waves since He created them, and He can glide right on top of them and come to us when we least expect it. In the natural, we have power to ride a wave, but in the supernatural, the power creates waves. Jesus can also calm those rough, turbulent waves, so even wake boards would be useless in the still, placid, and untroubled waters that now present an opportunity for a supernatural encounter with the Lord.

In some cases it appears that what we are experiencing may be the worst torrential flooding storm of our lives, and at other times it may seem more like a fire storm. Isaiah 43:2 shares this insight: "When you pass through the waters, I will be with you; and through the rivers, they shall not overflow you. When you walk through the fire, you shall not be burned, nor shall the flame scorch you."

So if you are going through hell, don't stop. Don't get a hotel or a condo there. Keep right on going. We don't simply go through things, but we need to understand that we go *through* things to go *to* something new. Psalm 23 shouts a victory position to us with the words, "Yea, though I walk through." And let me tell you right now, there are no water wells in hell. So you have to press on even in the mist of deep personal trial and sadness. You must keep fighting, even if you head is hanging low. Press on, my friend, as God is much nearer than you may presently realize.

Today, if you find yourself in a pitiful position with perhaps even your own condescending despondent tone of voice despairingly crying out, "Well, well, well, I wonder if this will end well," keep your eyes open, and look for Jesus to appear, because this could be the day. It has been said that Jesus is never early or late, but always punctual and right on time. I can assure you that Jesus is still very devoted to you just like He was the day He died and gave His life for you. Nothing has changed. He promises us that His Word is always valid and will never return void. His word is His bond.

Fourteenth Checkup: Supernatural Perseverance

Encouraging Response

Ephesians 6:13–18 says it this way in the Message Bible:

> Be prepared. You're up against far more than you can handle on your own. Take all the help you can get, every weapon God has issued, so that when it's all over but the shouting you'll still be on your feet. Truth, righteousness, peace, faith, and salvation are more than words. Learn how to apply them. You'll need them throughout your life. God's Word is an indispensable weapon. In the same way, prayer is essential in this ongoing warfare. Pray hard and long. Pray for your brothers and sisters. Keep your eyes open. Keep each other's spirits up so that no one falls behind or drops out.

It definitely is a great day to get well, and it absolutely is a day worth praising God for in the midst of your trials, troubles, problems, and roadblocks that may still be agitating and plaguing you. Keep talking to Jesus, as He never grows tired of communicating with you. Find something to be thankful for even in the midst of great pain, anguish, and perhaps sorrow.

And as you praise Him, don't be surprised if you hear the Lord respond back to you with an ascending tone of "Well, well, well, look at My child. There is My son, my daughter, praising Me even when it looks like all hope is lost." And through this, your internalized pain and hardships become externalized patterns of trust and rejoicing through His loving care. These realities of your walk with Jesus enable you to walk all the more closely with Him, as James 4 challenges us to submit to God and resist the devil, and then to draw near to God so He will draw near to you.

Right now, while I am physically, presently, and personally experiencing pain in my own body even as I write these final thoughts, I believe that God is working behind the scenes for me. He has always done it in the past, so there is no reason to doubt it now. He personifies true love for His children and writes our names in the Book of Life as a statement to the world that we belong to Him. We have been adopted into the family of God and truly are His sons and daughters.

I really do believe that God sees you in any distress you may experience and still comes directly to you with healing, provision, and solutions for what you presently need. He is not negligent in any way. He is, after all, Jehovah Rapha, the God Who heals. Yes, according to the Bible, there is an appointed time to die, but nowhere in the New Testament can you find that you should or will die sick. Most people think they will die in some form of sickness or illness because that is the norm of most of their friends, but the reality of the Word of God is that the abundant life is ours even to our last breath. Let's trust God for His best, rather than the world's worst. Besides I would rather aim high and miss it a little bit then aim low and make it.

There is a cartoon depicting Charlie Brown with a bow and arrow, shooting arrows at a fence. When the arrow hits the fence, Charlie Brown goes over and draws a circle around the arrow as if he hit the target dead center. Lucy comes over and observes this for a while and finally shouts out, "Charlie Brown, that's not how you do target practice," to which Charlie Brown responds, "I know, but if you do it my way, you never miss."

Second Corinthians 5:9 promotes this thought: "Therefore we make it our aim, whether present or absent, to be well pleasing to Him." Let me tell you, when we do it God's way, we never miss. You can circle that too. As I already stated, the word *sin* is an archery term that means missing the mark. When we are not obedient to God's instructions, we are in essence missing the mark. Occasionally, we must draw a big circle around our times of perseverance so that we stay on target with what Jesus is leading us to do. Jesus practiced this in the garden of Gethsemane when He cried out to His Father with the words, "Nevertheless, not My will, but Your will be done." He asked if there was another way, but He had to persevere to the Cross, which was the target that the Father asked Him to aim at.

Fourteenth Checkup: Supernatural Perseverance

Sometimes, we must also circle the aspect of perseverance in our lives through obedience to what the Father is asking us to do, rather than the quick fix that we would personally desire. Through self-control and godliness, that perseverance is accessed through His supernatural power. We don't always understand why we have to wait, but it is in those longer seasons of waiting that we choose to take Him at His Word and trust Him. Trust is a must!

And you probably thought I would somehow end with the words *well, well, well*.

Closing Prayers
By Jason West

A Prayer for Physical Healing for Others:

Father God, we thank You that You are the giver of all good things. Right now, we invite Your presence to come powerfully and manifestly into the lives of those in need of Your healing touch. We believe for You to work supernaturally to bring wholeness and health to their bodies wherever they are in need of Your Divine intervention. Whether the malady is visible or invisible, painful or pain-free, noticeable or unnoticeable, we declare healing to flow into their bodies. As they are reading this prayer, let this become a "now" word for them as they experience Your healing power even at this very moment. Thank You for what You're doing, Lord. We bless Your holy name.

A Prayer for Personal Healing:

Thank You, Lord, that You are my healer! Right now, I cast my cares upon You, for I know that You care for me. I ask and believe for You to heal my body from this sickness, disease, or infirmity. Only You can do this. Therefore, I boldly approach Your throne of grace and seek Your face, believing for supernatural intervention in my current situation. I praise You for doing this, and I am excited to testify of what You have done so that others may apply this testimony as a prophetic word to their current situation too. Thank You, Jesus, for healing me. I love You!

A Prayer for Restored Relationships:

> *Lord, You are a God Who restores. You bring healing out of brokenness, joy out of sorrow, and peace out of strife. Right now, we boldly come before you, claiming victory and restoration for those who are dealing with broken relationships. We pray for godly wisdom for them to know how to begin to mend that which was broken. We pray for supernatural grace to rest upon these people as they seek You for guidance and intervention in these relationships. Lord, bring unity out of chaos, calmness out of confusion, and life out of that which seemed dead prior to this point. We entrust all these things unto Your care. Thank you, Jesus!*

A Prayer for Financial Breakthrough:

> *Jehovah Jireh, You are our Provider. Everything we need, You have; and everything You have, we need. We now run to You and seek You on behalf of those who need a financial breakthrough in their lives. Only You can solve the problems they may be facing, and only You can provide an answer. Encourage them to trust You, no matter what the circumstances may be. Teach them to have faith that You truly do provide all that they need. We pray that whatever may have caused financial instability and lack in the past would now be broken off these people, in Jesus' name. We pray for financial victories to begin to occur and that the situation would begin to turn around this very day. We know that we can trust You with this, and we thank You for Your faithfulness in all things. Praise the Lord!*

Other Products Available from Anointed 2 Go MdM

Music CD

Running Free
Original Songs by Jason West
Suggested donation: $10

Books

Who Will Ascend?
Taking Prayer to Another Level
By Jason B. West
Suggested donation: $10

Kingdom Encounters
Keys to Unlocking God's Treasures
By Jay W. West and Jason B. West
Suggested donation: $12

Downloads from Heaven
Instructions and Examples of Hearing from God
By Jay W. West
Suggested donation: $10

Willing to Yield
Discover How "Yielding" Accesses the Supernatural Wisdom, Favor, and Power of God
By Jay W. West
Suggested donation: $10

Freedom through Surrender
A 31-Day Devotional
By Jason West

To order these and other products from Anointed 2 Go, please contact:

Jay at **anointed2go@cox.net**

or

Jason at **runningfree@cox.net**

Please note that minimal shipping costs will be added to each order, which vary slightly with each order.

Stay up to date with Anointed 2 Go by following Jay's blog at **http://anointed2go.com**

Follow Jason's blog at **http://chroniclesofprayer.wordpress.com**

Website for Kingdom Encounters **http://kingdomencounters.net**

Website for Anointed 2 GO MdM **http://anointed2go.net**

Notes

1. Beach Boys. "Catch a Wave." 1963.

2. "Origin of 'Well, Well, Well. What Do We Have Here?'" *English Language & Usage.* Etymology, 7 May 2012. Web. 15 July 2014.

3. *The Santa Clause 2.* Dir. Michael Lembeck. Perf. Tim Allen and Eric Lloyd. Walt Disney Pictures, 2002. DVD.

4. MaddogS. "Aye Aye." *Urban Dictionary.* N.p., 30 Sept. 2003. Web. 08 Aug. 2014.

5. Baloche, Paul. "Open the Eyes of My Heart." Integrity's Hosanna! Music (Admin. by EMI Christian Music Publishing (IMI)), 1997.

6. West, Jason B. "The Prayer of Power." *Who Will Ascend? Taking Prayer to Another Level.* Bellevue, NE. 2013. Print.

*Please note: This book has undergone two critical editing reviews, in which two different trained editors have thoroughly commented, critiqued, and corrected all the errors they could find. In addition to those reviews, I personally reexamined and inspected the book a third time for final polishing. However, despite our best efforts, we admit that catching every typo and every grammatical error is a very difficult, tedious, and time-consuming task to accomplish. We have done our best, but please be gracious if you still find an occasional lingering discrepancy. Thank you.

www.ingramcontent.com/pod-product-compliance
Lightning Source LLC
Chambersburg PA
CBHW070103080526
44586CB00013B/1166